The New Selfish

YOUR PATH TO FREEDOM

David Cavill

Table of Contents

Introduction 5
Your Story. 13
Knowing Yourself 34
Self-Acceptance 51
Living Authentically. 75
Attitude 91
Decision Making and Commitments 108
The Inward Journey Part 1 131
The Inward Journey Part 2 150
The Outward Journey. 169
50 Famous People Who Failed At First 185
Sources 199

Introduction

When I was nine years old, I lived in a small bungalow next to beautiful green fields in England with my mum, dad and two brothers. I loved soccer. Life was grand! I was dreaming of playing in a soccer game and scoring the winning goal when awakened by angry voices coming from the kitchen area of the house. Mum and dad were screaming at each other. Not accustomed to mum and dad fighting, I nervously walked towards the kitchen unsure of what I would see. I peeked through the crack of the door. Mum was gripping a butcher knife, the same knife she used to slice the Christmas day turkey. Her hand was shaking, tears flooding her face. My dad was screaming at her, his face red from rage. I pushed the door open. My mother and father froze, the knife making a loud clanging noise as it hit the floor. She ran past me into the hallway, sobbing as she grabbed her coat from the coat rack and ran out the front door. I chased after her as she ran down the driveway. I cried out, "Mum, please don't go!". It was pouring now, the icy wind sending shivers through my tiny body. The rain beat against my face as I ran up the road chasing after her, my pajamas the only protection against the icy wind. I was screaming in desperation. The woman I loved more than anything in the world was leaving me! "Mum, don't leave! Please don't go." Tears were flooding down my little freckled face. "Mum, don't leave! Please, don't leave!"

She stopped, kneeling down beside me as the rain and cold realization washed over me. She said the words I've never forgotten: "David, I have to go. One day you will understand." She gently kissed my forehead and then walked away. It turned out that mum was having an affair. My father, I later discovered, had asked her that morning to swear on her children's lives that she was not cheating on him. She couldn't lie, not to my dad, not to herself. She was in love with another man.

According to the Association for Psychological Science, studies show that we don't accurately remember details from childhood but fill in the blanks with our imagination. It was over 50 years ago that my mother left home. Did she really have a knife? Did she run out of the door that morning? Did I run up the road after her in my pajamas? I cannot swear to the facts. What I can tell you is that's the story I carried with me to every relationship, *but not consciously*. I know my mum left home that day, leaving my dad to raise three boys. It turned out that her love affair ended badly a few years later. My mother came from a broken home. She too, was a wounded, abandoned child telling herself a story similar to the one I have been telling myself for years.

People love to validate their beliefs and will do almost anything to justify what they believe. So much of what we do, we do in ignorance, born from a belief system that was never really ours to begin with. That day I inherited a belief that I could not trust a woman; that she would leave me. I learned not to value myself, that I was not lovable, attracting experiences to validate my unconscious beliefs; seeking short-term gratifications to avoid the feelings I didn't want to feel.

So many of us wounded in childhood don't value ourselves because of the messages we received growing up. Beliefs passed down through generational transference are adopted as truths that, when examined, are simply not true. Unable to trust in our own intelligence, disconnected from our source, we unconsciously tell ourselves a story; that we are not worthy, attracting like minds to confirm our beliefs. We act out of anger and abandonment, inflicting pain upon each other from a wounded past we had no control over. *"Please forgive them for they know not what they do"* were the words of Jesus as they nailed his hands and feet to the cross. If we truly valued ourselves, we would do things differently. We would invest the time and energy to be conscious of our thoughts and choices. We would take responsibility for our outcomes and investigate unconscious patterns in our lives that are not working.

The Old Selfish

The word "selfish" is defined as concerned excessively with oneself: seeking or concentrating on one's own advantage, pleasure, or well being without regard for others: arising from concern with one's own welfare or advantage. A selfish person is concerned about themselves and what they can achieve without regard for other people's wellbeing. The old selfish is about ego satisfaction and what's in it for me? In part, it's a survivorship mentality and how the human brain is wired. I better get mine before someone else does! In the bigger picture, it's a way to feel validated, to feel special, to prove worthiness. Disconnected from our true self, we chase what we think will make us feel whole: money, a love partner, and a fancy car, always something outside of ourselves. We keep chasing and yet no matter how much we gain in the world, it's never enough. The emptiness is inside of us, and nothing outside can fill the void for very long. The need for approval and recognition from a wounded past, fueled by inherited beliefs, causes much suffering in the world. Much of what we do, we do in ignorance, born from a belief system that was never really ours to begin with.

The New Selfish

The New Selfish is about setting yourself free from the need for approval or validation. You do what you do because you love yourself as that person, at a deep integral level. You no longer do what you do to be approved of or accepted by others, but because it feels congruent and right for you. When you do what's right for you, as a byproduct, it will also be right for others as well. By practicing the strategies in this book, you become a "Soul Toucher"; a light that shines brightly as you surrender to your true nature, touching others' souls, as your light grows ever brighter. What you give opens you to receive as love multiplies upon itself, expanding as the universe expands. It's within your higher nature to give; for it is in the giving that we open to the abundance that is always present and awaiting our surrender. From this place of self-acceptance, it's only natural then that we want to share our gifts with others. In order to share our self freely without attachments, we must develop our gifts and transform our story. Much the same as an entertainer who works tirelessly on their craft to share their gift, it is our responsibility to develop what lies within. We must value ourselves and do the work that will transform us into the powerful beings we are. We must do our part to join with the intelligence that desires expression by surrendering to a higher power that knows what's best, and learn to surrender to the force that is our human spirit. To find it, we must go within and know ourselves at a deeper, more intimate level. We need the faith and courage to express ourselves in the world through our unique expression of the life that dwells within. There is greatness in all of us. However, we must do the work! When you truly value yourself, the "work" is a labor of love that only you can do. You have a purpose for being here. It's up to you to discover what lies within, and then give of yourself without attachments or agendas.

Who Can Benefit From "The New Selfish?"

The New Selfish will teach you to live authentically without the need for approval from others. If you are constantly doing for others, serving them while you quietly suffer, but no matter what you do, it's never enough, then this book will help free you from the need for approval and teach you self-love.

If you suffer with anxiety, striving to make everything feel right for once in your life, that there's a feeling of emptiness within, "The New Selfish" can help you grow beyond the fearful patterns that are keeping you stuck.

In this book, you will learn tools to know yourself through "Camera Talk" and other suggested methods to help free you

The New Selfish

from toxic thinking. As you practice self-awareness, you naturally become more self-accepting, transforming your story to live an authentic life. By learning to monitor your attitudes and behaviors and what feels right for you, you discover that making intelligent decisions and commitments is the very thing that will set you free. This newfound freedom leads you to share yourself more fully with the outer world, where you naturally become the giver you were born to be. By working through the exercises in this book, you can embrace your story as a learning tool for yourself, and as a teaching tool for others, as you shine your light brightly to discover that freedom is but a breath away.

"The New Selfish" will show you how to...

- Understand inherited patterns from the past
- Utilize strategies to know yourself more intimately
- Accept yourself without judgment
- Live authentically
- Understand attitude is a strategy
- Make intelligent decisions
- Recognize commitment gives you freedom
- Use "Camera Talk" effectively
- Discover your purpose
- Release yourself from the need for other's approval
- Develop your gifts
- Give of yourself with self-love and confidence

CHAPTER 1

"Those that fail to learn from history are destined to repeat it."

Winston Churchill

Your Story

Events in previous generations can affect behavior, which have been passed on through a form of genetic memory, animal studies suggest. Experiments showed that a traumatic event could affect the DNA in sperm and alter the brains and behavior of subsequent generations. A nature neuroscience study shows mice trained to avoid a smell passed their aversion on to their "grandchildren". Experts said the results were important for phobia and anxiety research. They trained the animals to fear a smell similar to cherry blossom. The team at the Emory University School of Medicine, in the US, looked at what was happening inside the sperm. They showed a section of DNA responsible for sensitivity to the cherry blossom scent was made more active in the mice's sperm.

Both the mice's offspring, and their offspring, were "extremely sensitive" to cherry blossom and would avoid the scent, despite never having experienced it in their lives. They also found changes in brain structure. "The experiences of a parent, even before conceiving, markedly influence both structure and function in the nervous system of subsequent generations," the report concluded. The findings provide evidence of "trans generational epigenetic inheritance" - suggesting the environment can affect an individual's genetics, which can be passed on.

One researcher, Dr. Brian Dias, claims: This might be one mechanism that descendants show imprints of their ancestor, there is absolutely no doubt that what happens to the sperm and egg will affect subsequent generations."

Prof Marcus Pembrey, from University College London, said the findings were "highly relevant to phobias, anxiety and post-traumatic stress disorders" and provided "compelling evidence" that memory could be passed between generations.

Many types of molecular mechanisms can retain memories in biological systems, such as metabolic changes, epigenetic factors, stable bioelectrical circuit modes, or neuronal-circuits. For example, a decapitated flatworm (planarians) that grows a new head seems to retain memories from its old one. Over half a century ago, experiments by James McConnell at the University of Michigan suggested memory in flatworms could be transferred through cannibalism. A flatworm could learn the memories of another by eating it! When McConnell first began studying planarians in the 1950s, his colleagues didn't even believe they could condition invertebrates like rats or mice. He proved them wrong and took his experiments in ever more extraordinary directions.

The New Selfish

McConnell began by simply taking advantage of the flatworm's remarkable regeneration abilities by cutting them into tiny, barely visible pieces as small as 1/279, which regenerated into a complete creature! For his initial experiments on memory, McConnell simply chopped his conditioned planarian in two and tested the regenerated halves. They conditioned the original worm to associate light with an electric shock, twitching in response to the light even when no shock was given. The tail half, which had grown a new head, learned this association more quickly than an untrained planarian. In a follow-up experiment, he chopped regenerated planarians in half again and again, testing newly regenerated worms that did not contain any parts of the original trained worm. Still, these regenerated planarians retained some memory. McConnell began thinking that memories were encoded, not in the brain's structure but in individual molecules.

In more recent times, neuroscientist Oded Rechavi, an Israeli professor from the University of Tel Aviv, recognizes the flatworm is an ideal test subject because it only takes approximately 50 days to develop 14 generations. These studies leave clues about what's possible in other animals, including humans. The problem with studying genetic memory in humans is that it takes generations to develop and is therefore challenging to measure epigenetic inheritance. However, it appears powerful events in our lives can indeed affect the development of our children and perhaps even grandchildren. As an example, one study showed increased glucose intolerance in the children and grandchildren of women who survived the Dutch famine of 1944-45, and another study showed that descendants of Holocaust survivors have lower levels of the hormone cortisol, which helps your body bounce back after trauma. Nature wastes nothing in her attempt to pass down information to living organisms. It is her way of better equipping future generations to face the same environmental conditions as previous generations. The environment writes the story of our genes, and our DNA is the rich history book of generations untold. Science is just beginning to catch up in its understanding of nature's wisdom. It's time to contribute to the story by demonstrating altruistic traits and behaviors. As Joe Dispenza so eloquently states, "By loving one another and cooperating—instead of warring and living in constant fear—we just might outgrow Darwin's survival of the fittest, for "thriving with the wisest." In this chapter, I share stories from my past as examples to help you recognize your own patterns that may be an inheritance from your ancestry. My story and its unfolding begins with my mother.

My Story - Mum

My mum was the life of the party and loved by all who met her. She loved to tell stories of how people would compliment her on how she resembled Elizabeth Taylor, and she did! So much so that she adopted the same hairstyles and makeup as the famous actress. As a young girl, she was following in the footsteps of her parents, who were both in show business. She loved to sing and had dreams of being an entertainer. Unfortunately, the dream never became a reality. My mother met my dad at the Hoover factory in London, England, where they were both employed. My father, who was older, was an escape route from the shackles imposed by her mother, who was angry and controlling, herself wounded from her own abandoned past. Mum married dad when she was just 17 years old, becoming a stay at-home mum, giving birth to three sons, of which I was the middle child. I think so often it's true that when a woman marries a man that is significantly older; they are unconsciously searching for the father figure they never had. Later on in life, as the years pass, they realize that they never really loved the person they married, but the decision was based on false premises of safety and security, a means to run away from home and be an adult, no longer a child. This was when my mother left our family. She was 35 years old. Almost as returning to her teenage years, my mum had a burning desire to discover herself and explore the world. She landed a position in the ladies' fashion business, where she excelled. This newfound freedom exposed her to a new life where she met a business executive and fell in love. The problem was they were both married, and the relationship would end badly.

Children are great observers, but lousy interpreters. In my mind, as the abandoned child, I made my mother's decision to leave home about me. As an adult, I have been attracted to instability, whether it was circumstantial or emotional. It's not that the women I dated were all unstable, but the women I had "chemistry" with were aligning with my insecurities. My own feelings of inadequacy mirrored the instability and brokenness that I attracted; in the grip of my unconscious, unaware of repetitive patterns that were destructive, I was unknowingly attracting experiences to justify my beliefs that women are not to be trusted, that they would abandon me. I was still the wounded little boy and didn't know it. It was not until I was in my early 30s where I experienced a relationship break up that I realized I wasn't grieving the loss of my girlfriend, but the abandonment from my mother. I had never grieved my mother leaving home and was unaware of the pain and anger driving my life. It was through deep, painful grieving that I processed feelings I had kept buried for so long. This was when I began my experimentation with "Camera Talk", amongst other forms of therapy, uncovering the wounds that needed love and forgiveness.

The Ancestral Past

I had been living in Florida for several years when I returned to England to interview my parents and gain clarity on where the patterns in my life originated. If your parents are still alive, it's helpful to ask questions about their past as an interested observer without attachment to how their behaviors may have affected you. In order to do this effectively, it's helpful to understand that they were acting out from what they knew from their past. This attitude does not make what they may, or may not have done ok, or acceptable to the child that was you. But in order for you to become free, it's essential to remove your personal feelings for a sufficient time period so that you can understand where your parents were coming from. That you recognize the behaviors were not personal to you, but from an inherited past. It was their identity, but not who they really are! From these "interviews," I learned that my mother's father had abandoned her when she was a little girl. I was aware of this, but had never been interested in the details previously. As a younger man, I was too busy living my life to concern myself with such trivia. I think most of us when we are young are not aware of how our parent's past affects our own lives. Realizing their past literally infected me with fears of abandonment and loss, I was now very much interested in understanding why I viewed the world the way I did, and what actually happened to my parents in their

The New Selfish

past? During these conversations, I uncovered the reasons my parents made the choices they made. On the few occasions that my mother saw her father, she could not call him "dad". Her father, my granddad, was married to another woman and didn't want anyone knowing she was his daughter. My mother's parents, my grandparents, were entertainers who performed a comedy act at vaudeville theatres in seaside towns in England. Their act was called "This, That and The Other," a comedy act interspersed with my grandma's beautiful singing voice. While on their travels from theater to theater, my grandmother took time out from entertaining to give birth to two daughters, 14 years apart, both born out of wedlock. My mother was the youngest child. Shortly after my mother was born, my grandparents separated. My grandmother could no longer continue to live the lifestyle that was required to be a traveling entertainer with another young child in tow. And so the story goes, my grandfather went back to his wife in Yorkshire, England. My mum barely knew her dad and felt this deep sense of abandonment, even though she would never admit it. My mother was really great at pretending that everything was OK. Her famous motto was "never look back". It's a great motto; however, if you haven't healed the wounds from the past, they will resurface. It's inevitable, because it's energy! At seventeen years of age, my mother left her mother's home, which she likely blamed unconsciously for not having a father, to marry my dad who represented what she never had; a stable male energy that she could trust. Eighteen years after she married dad, she left. She was still young, and was tired of the routine and her marriage. The stable man she married was no longer interesting. My mother passed down to us what she had experienced through her own unconscious energy, which was abandonment. We seek it out and it comes right back to us, all without our knowing. I loved my mother; she was the star in her children's eyes. We all loved her so much that it still hurts. It is from the deepest wounds that true healing can occur. It's a rite of passage that we must all take if we truly want to feel free and live our own authentic life. If my mother had not left our home in England, I'm sure I would have never moved to America, and certainly would not be writing this book. We are all responsible for transforming our story and recognizing the healing that can come when we embrace what has happened. My mother didn't leave home because she no longer cared about her children; she left home because she had to.

Dad

My Dad was a kind, caring man who also carried his own wounds from a tough childhood. He was the youngest of 8 children who never received love and attention from his mother because she was exhausted from having to take care of so many kids. They were also very poor, which only made her responsibilities more difficult. My dad's father had died when he was just three years old, whereupon his mum married an alcoholic who abused her. Dad related stories where he physically fought his stepfather over the mistreatment of his mum. He was proud that, even though much smaller in stature, he stood up to his stepfather to protect his beloved mother against incessant abuse, because in his words, "she was so worn out". His siblings were disrespectful and also abusive to her. Over the years, after joining the Army for World War 2, he would become his mum's protector. Dad loved women in the most respectful of ways, unknowingly searching to not only feel loved by a woman, but also to protect her. They had perfect chemistry, unknowingly matching each other's needs. Mum was seeking a father figure, and dad was looking for a woman he could protect. I'm sure that if I could look into the kaleidoscope of my ancestral past, I would likely see similar patterns in the evolution of my lineage. The unlikely story of my daughter Georgina exemplifies the energy patterns that persist from generation to generation. It is our responsibility to wake up from these energetic patterns and break the habits from the past.

Georgina

My English friend Steve had invited me to play golf with his University buddy Dean who was visiting from England. I was in a desperate state in my life as my ex-girlfriend was six months pregnant, dealing with the emotions of knowing that I could not marry her, and the painful realization that she was moving to her home state of Ohio, meaning I would not see my child, and dealing with the added pain of paying child support. I had been isolating, while berating myself for my decisions, unaware of the anger and abandonment from my childhood and how I unconsciously inflicted my anger on the women in my life, incapable of sustaining a relationship because of my need to prove myself, not recognizing I was objectifying women to feed my ego, misogynistic, unaware of the buried pain from my abandonment issues. I wanted to prove myself; that I was loveable, special, and all the things I never believed, desperately needing to feel good about myself, because I didn't, addicted to the energy patterns from a wounded past. While playing golf, Steve's friend Dean explained he was visiting with his girlfriend, but they were no longer a couple? Apparently, he had met a young woman in the UK and was anxiously waiting to see his new love upon his return. I asked why he had still come on the trip with his current girlfriend if he was so besotted with this other young woman? He explained they were traveling together as they had already purchased their tickets some months previously, and had remained friends for their holiday. The explanation sounded a little off to me, but who cares? I thought. I had enough of my stuff, or did I? When we finished playing golf, we made our way to the clubhouse to have a beer and relax. Steve's wife and his friend Dean's girlfriend, Paula, entered the clubhouse. Our eyes locked! Time stood still. My life would never be the same.

She was a beautiful 25-year-old girl from Yorkshire, England, as lovely on the inside as she was on the out, reminding me of the home I never had. I was completely smitten and totally unaware not wanting to know of the toxic relationship that she was currently involved in with Dean. The drama had begun. The chemistry was immediate and palpable. Neither of us could take our eyes off each other. Dean was a muscular brute of a fellow and not someone I would want to tangle with. It's amazing what we will do when the force of chemistry is propelling us into an abyss that we do not want to see. Over the three-week period, we became deeply involved, hiding the affair from Dean with the help of Steve's wife. Dean was abusive, treating Paula disrespectfully, ignoring her, and constantly making sarcastic remarks. He was full of ego, not realizing his ugly behavior. Steve's wife wanted to help free Paula, knowing that she was deeply unhappy, clandestinely encouraging our secret meetings. Enter David, the dragon slayer, ready to save the day, the rescuer on his white horse - "Lancelot" eager to save his damsel in distress, my ego driving me into the abyss of "LOVE", unknowingly involving myself in heavy drama. I had a love / hate relationship with women, which I was completely unaware. Paula and I were imbedded in the wounded past, both destined to pay a heavy price for the affair.

Pie In My Face

Prior to our affair and a few days after playing golf, Dean invited me to go along with himself and Paula to MGM Studios together with my friend Steve and his wife. Dean was unconsciously feeding his own pain body, attracting the saboteur to remind him of his own beliefs. We were all actors in our own personal drama, unaware of the damaging actions being played out from a distant past. One show at MGM studios was a live presentation where they chose people from the audience to show how entertainment of the past was enacted. They chose me from the audience to play a role in the "Three Stooges". The members of the show escorted me backstage, where I was made ready for action, dressed in a tuxedo, to play the part of an English Butler. During the scene, they directed one of the Three Stooges to throw a cream pie into his adversary's face; who was standing directly in front of me? As the cream pie was thrown, his adversary ducked. I was the recipient of a cream pie smashing into my unsuspecting face. As I wiped away the sticky mess from my eyes, I peered through the stage lights to see Paula, Dean, and the audience uproariously laughing. I did not know what a metaphor that was to be! I was the Stooge in my play, and didn't know it.

The Wedding

One month after Paula left Florida, I visited her in England, where we attended a close friend's wedding. My friends Martin and Nicky were getting married. During the month after we had met, Paula had left her boyfriend Dean as promised, and had moved back home to live with her parents. We were planning on being together and for her to move to Florida. It was a beautiful sunny English day as the wedding party and guests entered the old English Church. When I enter these old historic buildings where so many have come before, for a moment I can sense the wholeness of life and how transient it all is. All the pain, tears, suffering, joy and laughter that so many felt while in this hallowed place, many of which are laid to rest on the church grounds. Ralph Waldo Emerson said; "I like the silent church before the service begins, better than any preaching." After entering the church, Paula and I sat towards the back of the sanctuary along with an old friend who I'd worked with in the casino business named Greg. He was one of the funniest people I've ever known. Greg was also a fantastic disco dancer with moves so phenomenal that he had won several disco dancing competitions. Unfortunately, he was also a raging alcoholic and so we sat at the back of the Church, just in case?

Meanwhile, at the front of the Church were Martin and Nicky about to make their nuptials. Martin reminded me of my father, who loved women for all the right reasons. His own father was an alcoholic who had abused his mother. Nicky had come from a single-family home, her mother a strong, determined businesswoman had raised her. Her father was in her life, but not the dominant figure. Nicky's father was a tall, kind, sweet man, much the same as Martin in demeanor and stature. I would ask at this point in the story that you please pay close attention to what transpires, because it's an extreme example of the patterns that we live in and the ensuing pain that can result. As Martin began his vows, women in the front pews sniffled, as women do at weddings. Martin's voice cracked as he fought back his own emotions; the joy of marrying his beautiful bride was almost too much for him to bear. And this was the moment I shall never forget: Greg, already in a drunken state from early morning vodkas, turned to Paula and myself, imitating the ladies crying at the front of the church. His facial expressions were that of an animated cartoon character that we simply could not resist. The three of us sank below the old English church pews like naughty school children suppressing our laughter. I was doing my best to be the responsible one and quiet him down, but it was impossible not to laugh at such a clown. My stern face only magnified the giggling, making the situation all the worse. From my low position I snuck my head into the gangway to witness the disgruntled wedding guests shaking their heads disagreeably, looking back in our direction. Who were the nasty, invisible people giggling at such a beautiful and romantic moment?

We were the players and directors in our own play, unknowingly starring in an absurd comedy / drama that would take over three acts to have a happy ending. Our lives were never to be the same again. Eight short months after the marriage, Nicky left Martin for another man. Martin quit his job to spend several months staying with me in Florida. It took him several years to recover. The man Nicky fell in love with, a handsome Australian business executive, who worked in the newspaper business, she later discovered, was engaged to another woman in Australia.

The New Selfish

She also came to visit with me in Florida. When we are deeply wounded, it is the perfect time to begin transformation, when the world as we know it shatters. It is in these precious painful moments that change occurs, because we are in the unknown. The old paradigms of unconscious thinking are no longer working, forcing us to surrender, seeking anything to release us from the incessant pain. We become the wounded child seeking the love of a caring parent. It is the worst of times and the best of times. It is being in the belly of the whale, the night of the dark soul, and the perfect opportunity for change. In these difficult periods lies the opportunity to free ourselves from old wounds. It is in these times where the pain is so great that the portal to our soul opens that we can know our self more intimately. The old inherited wounds have a chance to breathe, to feel the healing power of deep love and grief, as we learn to let go of the "gift" albeit wrapped in "shitty wrapping paper".

Unbeknown to Paula and myself at that very moment, while giggling like naughty children under the church seats, was a little baby girl growing inside the womb of Paula. For 10 years, we assumed the father of her daughter was Dean, the boyfriend I played golf with on that fateful day. Just a few short months after the wedding, Paula went back with Dean to give birth to their daughter. She was, in fact, at that very moment, pregnant with my daughter Georgina. I was the father of her child, of whom I was unaware for 10 years. The following day, Paula and myself drove Greg, still drunk from the wedding party from the night before, to the railway station where he boarded a train to his destination, a small town in Czechoslovakia, where he worked for several years managing a casino. This is where he met his future wife, Sabina. Several years later, I heard through the grapevine they had given birth to a son named "little Greg". I also heard that Greg had stopped drinking. I remember thinking, "miracles happen!" Unfortunately, the rumor was not true. The entertaining charismatic disco dancing Greg that we all loved died a few years later of bone marrow cancer at the tender age of 39, in a hospital bed in Vienna, Austria. He always said he would never make it to 40, and he was right. After Greg's death, I received a phone call from Martin, who was now living with his new wife in Canada. Sabina, Greg's widow and her son, "little Greg" was staying with Martin and his new wife and baby. Martin was busy opening a new casino and had asked if I would visit to help Sabina through the grieving process. And so more drama began. I visited Martin, his wife Andrea, Sabina and "little Greg" in Canada, and the rest, as they say, is history. Three years later, still unaware that I had a daughter in England named Georgina, I married Sabina, where I became the stepfather to Greg's son. While we were laughing under the church pews, as Martin was pushing back tears of joy, his marriage to beautiful Nicky would end in less than a year. Paula was to be the future mother of my daughter Georgina and would endure much slander and pain, accused in her small town of being a whore, when they discovered Dean was not the father of her daughter a decade later. I was to become the father of a child I would not know for 10 years. I would also become the future husband of Greg's widow and play the role of his son's stepfather until a better choice would appear. All this happened out of our unconscious energy! What tangled webs we weave!

Patterns

For a decade, it was assumed the father of Georgina was Dean, who I played golf with on that beautiful sunny day in Florida. I received a phone call from Paula one day proclaiming Georgina was my daughter. I arranged for a DNA paternity test, confirming I was Georgina's biological father. Once I received confirmation, I flew to the UK and visited her in Barnsley, Yorkshire. She was family, and it felt that way. I could never be the father she really needed and we have both suffered the consequences. Ironically, after discovering she was my daughter, Paula was working for the UK government in the registrations of births and deaths in her local constituency. Out of curiosity, she had investigated my ancestry. What we discovered was beyond anything we could have ever imagined. My daughter Georgina was born a few miles away from my grandfather's home in Yorkshire, and just a few miles from where my mother was born in Rotherham, Yorkshire. Georgina was conceived in Florida, and yet born a stone's throw from where my grandfather lived and where my mother was born! Georgina was born a few miles away from my Granddad who had abandoned his daughter, my mother. Here was history repeating itself! I was born many miles away from Yorkshire in the southwest part of England and had never visited the Yorkshire area ever in my life. My mother never really knew her father, and my daughter Georgina doesn't know me well either. If these patterns were artwork, how would they look? It still feels incredulous to me that all this could've occurred unconsciously. We were actors in a drama that was being played out from the energy patterns of our past. "The path to truth with closed eyes will always be painful!"

Awareness

When examining our behaviors and the ensuing effects, with greater awareness, we can free ourselves from the same, or similar, patterns that continue to show up in our life. By discovering whom we are, and why we do what we do, we can make more conscious decisions. As we learn to value ourselves, we can align with the energy source that wants to free us, because the truth always sets us free. The truth may at sometimes be painful, much the same as bursting a cyst; however, once the negative energy drains from the wound, healing occurs. Whenever you feel an uneasy energy around a certain subject or particular question, this is an alert to inform you that you have an issue around whatever the subject or question may be? If you feel awkward around a certain subject or question, instead of closing down, or defending or attacking, remain open as an interested observer so you may attain more clarity.

The key to awareness is to be an interested observer, not minding being observed. As you become interested in your own and other's patterns, you gain more understanding why you attracted the circumstances and experiences that were painful. We are like magnets and mirrors, constantly attracting that what we most need to feel and see. Painful experiences take us deeper within, where we can release that which is old and toxic, strengthening our self to a new way of being. If we can have the courage to take an honest assessment of ourselves, without condemnation and judgment, we can live a happier and more fulfilled life. As the process of self-awareness and understanding permeates the unconscious mind, it's only natural then that we forgive both others and ourselves, recognizing we only knew what

The New Selfish

we knew and were acting out of our state of awareness, which very often is programming from the past. We realize the painful experiences were gifts that came in "shitty wrapping paper". By knowing yourself intimately, you can unhook from the toxic energies inherited from the ancestral past. You don't have to go through your entire life being at the mercy of an unconscious energy pattern that only knows suffering as a teaching tool. By taking the actions recommended in this book, you can free yourself to be the energy source that God intended you to be; not a slave from the past.

By allowing yourself to wake up to your story, you can use your story as a teaching tool to free yourself and others. You are on a hero's journey to assimilate, and where possible, embrace your past, because it has made you who you are! It is from your story that teaching and healing can occur. When you recognize your purpose as a healing force, and develop your gifts out of self-value, and then share those gifts with others from a place of authenticity and non-attachment, is when the life that you unconsciously have led so far will make sense. It is time to become conscious of your journey. No matter how strenuous life can be, there is a silver lining that permeates your story. If you use it, it will set you free! Knowing yourself is the gift that gives from what it knows. In order to unhook from the energy patterns that unconsciously drive our lives, we must understand our self at a deeper, more intimate level. The energy that lives deep within our psyche when transformed not only gives us freedom but may also free our ancestors stuck in the patterns from long ago.

In the Stephen Spielberg movie "Amistad" based on the true story of the uprising of slaves aboard the ship La Amistad in1839, Cinque, the slave leader says to John Quincy Adams, played by

The New Selfish

Anthony Hopkins, prior to the Supreme court trial resulting in the freeing of the slaves and the beginning of the end of slavery: "I will call into the past, far back to the beginning of time and beg them to come and help me at the judgment. I will reach back and draw them into me, and they must come. For at this moment I am the whole reason they have existed at all". The Supreme Court justices understood that men are created equal, consequently freeing Cinque and his fellow tribe members. His courage, and that of the former President John Quincy Adams, his defending attorney, was the beginning of the abolition of slavery, which would eventually lead to civil war. Your ancestors were slaves to their ignorance, to the conditions of the time, and the environment they had little control over. What your forefathers passed down through the generations was what they knew from their own limited awareness. One by one, they also suffered from an inherited past capable only of giving what they themselves could receive. It is because of ignorance of the universal laws that we experience pain and suffering, forcing us to contemplate our life, which results in our own evolution. Each generation can improve upon the last through recognizing patterns that are mostly inherited. Your story can have transformative benefits not only for you but also for those who can learn from your story.

Action Steps:

Talk to your camera or journal

1. If possible interview your parents. Ask them details about their upbringing. Be an interested observer looking for clues why they are the way they are?

2. How has your story affected those closest to you? Don't judge yourself! Journal, or talk to your camera. You can learn about "Camera Talk" in chapter 7, "The Inward Journey Part 1".

3. What has your childhood shown you NOT to do? What did your parents model for you that you could do differently?

4. What do you want to emulate from your parents or caretakers?

Because I know the Soul of You

Because I know the soul of you
The things you say that make me mad and sad
The times you misjudge me
And do not clearly see from some background mirror
That fogs the truth of who I am and want to be

Because I know the soul of you
These things that do infuriate me
These allegations that do bind me to me
Seem nothing when compared to the soul I know you to be
Seem nothing when I look beyond the behavior tree…
To the root, to the soul of you
At back of all you say and do
That sweet soul in full view

Even in rage and anger
All is forgotten when I think of the sweet soul… in you
That sweet soul of you
That does make all things small
That does not matter
And all things small that do
My annoyance in comparison…
Like an Englishman saying… Toodledooh!

CHAPTER 2

"This above all: to thine own self be true,
And it must follow as the night the day,
Thou canst not then be false to any man".

Shakespeare

Knowing Yourself

The term "metacognition" is an awareness of one's thought processes and an understanding of the patterns behind them. It involves knowing when you know, knowing when you don't know, and knowing what to do when you don't know. Metacognition is a major contributor to self-knowledge, and an underappreciated tool for improving thought efficiency. You are the expert of your own being. You are in charge of your thoughts and you are your own personality. By knowing who you are and what you stand for in life can help to give you a strong sense of self-confidence and independence, the ability to show empathy towards others, experience less conflict, and will help you discover your purpose. We are at a time in world history where there is a tremendous

The New Selfish

amount of division and uncertainty. The world has always been an uncertain place with economic depressions, wars, genocide, revolutions, and diseases. We are witnessing the evolution of humanity and the planet every day on the news and the Internet. Most of what we witness daily is scary stuff. And yet we are also at the precipice of incredible technological changes, presenting tremendous opportunities. On one side of the equation, the human family is being threatened, sometimes with extinction from our own man-made weapons and ignorance of universal laws. And yet out of the chaos comes great opportunities to prosper. The technological changes taking place in the world will make many people wealthy, including you and me, if we know how to think strategically without erroneous fears and trepidations. This is the human condition that we currently live within. It is both scary and exciting. The question then becomes which side of the coin do you want to live on? Do you want to focus on your fears, doubts and insecurities? Or commit to live an abundant life, developing your inherent gifts to experience purposeful living. The journey you are on is both challenging and exciting. Taking positive, purposeful actions is the only way to live the quality of life you deserve. If we are going to overcome the many obstacles life challenges us with, we must find our own path to happiness by making the commitments to take responsibility for our own lives. To be a part of the solution, we must take our rightful place in the universe by living our lives on purpose and freeing ourselves from the madness that entraps us.

In the previous chapter, we discussed the importance of seeking to understand the past and the patterns passed down through generational transference. In this chapter, I encourage you to investigate your nature through personality profiling, so you may understand your communication preferences and how you interact with others, and also to continue to examine adopted beliefs from childhood. As you realize your innate nature and recognize inherited patterns from the past, you naturally become more self-accepting. No longer confused and frustrated, you can free yourself by consciously choosing what to focus on and why. With a little guidance and your participation, you discover the answers are inside you. My goal is to help you uncover the answers for yourself, and discover who you are, and your purpose for being here. The world needs more consciously aware leaders.

Freeing Yourself

In order to free you from negative behavior patterns, it is helpful to know yourself to experience more conscious awareness. Knowing yourself is essential to accepting yourself. Self-acceptance is where the journey to change and purposeful living begins. As Socrates exclaimed, "An unexamined life is not worth living". If this book is to be of service to you, other than a potentially enjoyable read, commitment to going deeper within to increase your awareness of self is necessary. To know you is to love you. The adage that you have to love yourself first stands true! Committing to going within on your spiritual path and to the actions necessary in the outer world to discover your limitations and overcome them can be challenging. As you progress on your journey, the work becomes a way of life and a labor of self-love. If commitment is a scary word, and you need motivation to change, ask yourself how is what you're currently doing working in your life? Are you happy? Are you living your life on purpose? Do you have passionate reasons to get out of bed in the morning? Or are you just going through the motions day-by-day, week-by-week? How motivated are you to overcome your old self and live a purposeful life? If you want to jump forward to chapter 6, "Decision Making and Commitments", it may help you understand why making intelligent commitments is necessary for your freedom. It's perfectly normal to resist change, because as you already know, human beings are creatures of habit. If you think it's easy for a caterpillar to become a butterfly, watch the process on a nature channel and you probably agree that change is indeed difficult. However, when you come out of the other side, the hard work is worth it. For genuine change to occur, you must leverage yourself by taking consistent actions to overcome old patterns and venture into unexplored territories to increase awareness.

Nature

Knowing yourself and accepting yourself are synonymous with each other. It's helpful that we understand the importance of knowing our self intimately to experience greater self-acceptance. The more we can know ourselves, the more likely we are to accept who we are. There are two major elements to understanding yourself at a deeper and more intimate level, which is firstly your nature, and secondly how you were nurtured as a child. Regarding your nature, it is helpful to understand your strengths, preferences and attitudes in how you experience the world. For example, are you an introvert or an extrovert? Do you get energy from being around people, or do you recharge by being alone? How do you process information? Are you more likely to be intuitive, trusting your intuition, or more likely to be a person basing your decisions on practicality? How do you decide? Do you decide based on logic and what's primarily in it for you, or do you decide based on values and how you feel? How do you organize your life? Are you a methodical person, organized and punctual, or more relaxed in your organizational skills? Understanding your nature can help you understand and accept yourself and others, and improve your communication skills, which naturally leads to being an effective leader.

Frank

When I was in my 20s, I lived in the Bahamas, working in the casino business. While dealing blackjack one evening, I met a gentleman who was a homebuilder. I wanted to buy a home in Florida, which I planned to use as a rental property. Because I was unsure of the legal processes, I contacted an attorney referral program that gave me the name of a gentleman who was a contract attorney for real estate and family law. After viewing the property, I contacted his office for the closing. After arriving in Tampa, I drove to my new attorney friend Frank Natters office where we proceeded to the closing at a local bank. On the 25-minute drive, I learned more about myself from this man than anyone I'd ever met! After asking a few questions, he seemed to know everything about me? I was amazed how he could know so much, having just met me a few moments previously. After the closing, Frank and I visited a local coffee shop where he explained the Myers-Briggs personality type indicator.

He discussed how he had conspired with Isabel Myers-Briggs, who, along with her mother, was the founders of the MBTI. His knowledge astounded me. I wanted to know what he knew and understand others and myself more intimately. I recognized the power of communicating more effectively and was hungry to know more. Frank was a unique attorney who was never about the money. He was the antithesis of lawyer jokes, a kind man ever seeking to help people. When couples would visit his office seeking divorce, he would explain their personality types and their differences, often saving their marriage, but in the process would lose a paying customer. A few years after meeting Frank and now living in Florida, I went through a divorce and used his services for the proceedings. Unfortunately, my marriage was not one he could save. Feeling lost and alone, I asked Frank if we could set up seminars to help people understand themselves through the MBTI. I was searching for answers in my life and felt it would be a healthy way to enjoy community with people also challenged with understanding themselves and others.

We began weeknight and weekend sessions where people could learn about themselves and understand why they did what they did, and why their spouses and children behaved the way they did as well. It was always fun and enlightening. People love to learn about themselves and their loved ones. A few years later we gave seminars on cruise ships contracting with Celebrity cruise line, titling the name of our seminar "Discover Your Celebrity Personality". I later continued my relationship with Celebrity as a lecturer on self-hypnosis. All from a random phone call to an attorney referral service to buy a house! You never know who you're going to meet and why? Life unfolds without us having to understand the deeper meanings. We have to trust. Without trust, we have no foundation on which to build a purposeful life.

Personality Profiling

Personality type indicators are a useful tool to shine a light on your more natural ways of being in the world, so you can understand and accept yourself and others. Hopefully, by having more information, we are less likely to be judgmental. The more we can understand our self and accept our ways of being, the less confusion we will live in. Gaining knowledge about yourself and others is not to have more control, but so you may learn how to let go more easily of what you think life is supposed to look like from your narrow perspective. By opening ourselves to a wider view of life and appreciating differing points of view, we open the portal to receive through greater awareness. Mastering our attitudes through understanding differences between yourself and others can only improve the quality of our lives and those around us. By understanding our personality traits, we are less likely to judge as we learn to appreciate differences. When we can embrace our strengths and work on the weaker, less familiar areas of our personality, we become more self-aware. As Jane Fonda quotes, "We are not supposed to be perfect, but we are supposed to be whole".

Myers Briggs

The MBTI identifies individuals as having one of 16 personality types. The goal of the MBTI is to allow people to explore and understand their own personalities, including their likes, dislikes, strengths, weaknesses, career preferences, and compatibility with other people. No one-personality type is better than another. It isn't a profiling system looking for dysfunction or abnormality, but to help you learn about yourself and your inherent nature. The MBTI is based on four different evaluations. A simple explanation of the Myers-Briggs theory says there are two ways that we meet the world, either through extroversion or introversion. Extroverts go out and meet the world, whereas introverts wait for the world to come to them. Once we are out in the world, we take in information. According to the theory, we take in information through our five senses, which is called sensing, or through our sixth sense, which is called intuition. As we gather information, we decide based on the information we are processing. The theory suggests we make decisions based either through our thinking logical mind, or via our feeling, value-based decision-making process. And last, once we have made a decision, we organize our life based on judging, who prefers structure, and perceptive types, who prefer less structure. Below explains the differences according to the Myers-Briggs theory, understanding that we practice all the below explanations to some extent. The MBTI suggests we prefer one preference to the other, which is our stronger choice, thus leading to the four letters that make up our personality type profile.

Extraversion (E) - Introversion (I)

The differences between Extroverts and Introverts are a way to describe how people respond and interact with the world around them. While these terms are familiar to most people, the way in which they are used in the Myers Briggs indicator differs somewhat from their popular usage.

Extraverts are more outward engaged and tend to be more action-oriented, enjoy more frequent social interaction, and feel energized after spending time with other people. Introverts are inner focused and tend to be more thought-oriented, enjoy deep and meaningful social interactions, and feel recharged after spending time alone. Extraverts gain their energy by being around people. Introverts need alone time to reflect and recharge.

Sensing (S) - Intuition (I)

This scale involves looking at how people gather information from the world around them. Just like with extraversion and introversion, all people spend some time sensing and intuiting depending on the situation. According to the MBTI, people tend to be dominant in one area or the other. People who prefer sensing tend to pay a great deal of attention to reality, particularly to what they can learn from their own senses. They tend to focus on facts and details and enjoy getting hands-on experience. Those who prefer intuition pay more attention to things like patterns and impressions. They enjoy thinking about possibilities, imagining the future, and developing abstract theories.

Thinking (T) - Feeling (F)

This scale focuses on how people decide based on the information that they gathered from their sensing or intuition functions. People who prefer thinking place a greater emphasis on facts and objective data. They tend to be consistent, logical, and impersonal when weighing a decision. Those who prefer feeling are more likely to consider people and emotions when arriving at a conclusion.

Judging (J) - Perceiving (P)

The final scale involves how people deal with the outside world. Those who lean toward judging prefer structure and firm decisions. People who lean toward perceiving are more open, flexible, and adaptable. These two tendencies interact with the other scales. Remember, all people at least spend some time engaged in extraverted activities. The judging-perceiving scale helps describe whether you behave like an extravert when you are taking in new information (sensing and intuiting) or when you are deciding (thinking and feeling).

I profile as an INTP. I'm an introverted, intuitive, thinking, perceptive type. My type takes a long time to let people into their life, and an even longer time to let them go. They also have fewer friends, but deeper friendships. I'm also a thinking type, which means I make my best decisions based on logic. If I did not know these personality traits about myself, I would be more likely to judge myself when I'm unable to let something go as quickly as an extrovert, or if I'm not as heartfelt sometimes in my communication. Because I'm introverted, I have felt uncomfortable speaking to large groups of people, and am more at ease, one on one, or with small groups. In order to overcome these debilitating traits, I took acting lessons and public speaking classes. I also tried my hand at stand up comedy, comedy improvisation and hypnosis presentations along with hosting local TV cable and radio shows, all to overcome deeply rooted insecurities not only from my past but also from predisposed tendencies based on my knowledge of the MBTI. Understanding the need to stretch myself, I have done the opposite of what I was comfortable with, and have taken chances of myself, because I understood at a deeper level that negative feelings towards myself didn't have to stay the way they were. I have learned to accept my feelings of inadequacy were not actually who I was and weren't negative if I understood why I felt insecure. I slowly learned to let go of insecurities that had kept me stuck by practicing that what I was afraid of. If you are an introvert, then you can practice extroverted activities to grow beyond your comfort zone, as I have done. Many outstanding actors are introverts; because of an acute ability to observe, introverts can transform themselves into various characters at will and overcome their insecurity. Extroverts can practice more alone time through meditation, reading a book, along with other methodologies to feel more grounded. If you're an intuitive person, you can practice being present and aware of your senses by taking walks in nature to enjoy the present moment, which leads to a greater feeling of gratitude. Intuitive type people spend 75% of their life thinking of the future, stuck in their heads. Conversely, if you prefer sensing and are more practical, you can use your imagination for possibility thinking outside of the traditional box. Having this knowledge about your nature not only leads to more self-acceptance but also can help to strengthen the weaker, less familiar areas of your personality, and therefore be a more effective communicator. By understanding our personality traits, we are less likely to judge as we learn to appreciate and respect differences. We can embrace our strengths and work on the weaker, less familiar areas of our personality profile to become self-aware. If you want to know yourself on an intimate level regarding your nature, and if you haven't done so already, I suggest learning about your personality type. I like the Myers-Briggs indicator; there are many such other choices available on the Internet.

Nurture

As children, we don't have a filter for the experiences we observe. Children interpret their observations as meaningful and personal. For example, they may see mom and dad fighting and think that's what love is. These interpretations become patterns in adult life and adopted as beliefs. The abused "child" attracts an abusive partner, matching their beliefs. And on it goes, depending on the observations made in childhood. As discussed in chapter 1, we can pass behavior patterns on from generation to generation. The human brain is an incredibly complex system, a part of which is known as the reticular activation system, or RAS. The RAS is hyper focused on a specific belief or idea and will cut out all the noise not relevant to that idea or belief. It is a guidance system that focuses on what it believes it should focus on. If you focus on the bad things, then negativity will show up in your life. Conversely, if you focus on the good things and the potential for happiness and joy, then those experiences are more likely to show up in your life as well. That is why we get what we focus on and become what we think about. People love to be right and confirm what they believe. Squirrels gather nuts and people gather evidence! We will seek evidence, however trivial the evidence may be, to validate our beliefs, often, that is harmful and self-sabotaging to our own wellbeing.

Beliefs

Good salespeople understand we love two things the most, the sound of our name, and the need to be RIGHT. We will do almost anything to justify our beliefs! Few people actually examine why they believe what they believe, and have no clue what they believe and why? This is one of the main reasons we live in a mad world! I hope you can see how important it is for you to examine your beliefs, to know yourself more deeply and employ the RAS to guide you towards new frontiers and leave old patterns behind. Fortunately, scientist has discovered that the brain has neuroplasticity, which means it can change its focus through the ability of the brain to learn and grow through re-organization of the neural pathways, and consequently adopt new beliefs and attitudes by growing new neural connections. By continuing to learn and have an open mind, we can change what we believe, and therefore change what we attract into our life experience. You can reprogram your brain by adopting new attitudes that shift your perspective on what's important and why. Learning about yourself and practicing new habits is the key to freedom. Assimilating learning into actions and the resulting feelings is how you change what you attract. What we believe about men, women, relationships, money and other areas of our life are programs from the past. Our environment conditioned us. If you've lived long enough, and you are not 100% unconscious, over time and with reflection, you can recognize behavior patterns. I have lived long enough that when I look back on my relationships, I can see exactly how I have tried to keep safe and consequently have kept myself from having more intimate, open and more satisfying relationships. I can see who I have attracted and why. It's not possible to live a whole life if you are not conscious of the part you are playing in it! In attempts to gather more awareness around my dysfunction, I have taken part in talk therapy, group therapy, hypnotherapy, breath work, EMDR, plant medicine and many weekends, and weeklong workshops. I have learned

I can be my own best therapist if I can put space between my thoughts and behaviors. The tools recommended in this book can help speed the process of self-awareness, and consequently make you a more effective communicator, both for yourself and for those around you.

Freedom

How do you feel when you express yourself? The feeling of authentic expression is the feeling of freedom. We all know, for example, how pathetic it is to watch someone dancing when they are totally stiff and self-conscious. Most people, especially in western cultures, have a strong desire to have more money: it's not the accumulation of numbers in a bank account, but the feeling that you will have more freedom and worthiness to do whatever you want to do when you want to do it. This is what we would define as abundance. If you have more money in your bank account, but you don't have your health, then you don't have physical freedom; therefore, the abundance is negated by your health. If you have physical health and money, but suffer with anxiety, then the money and physical health are nullified when trapped in your own mind. As most people will suffer from some kind of physical challenge, mental anxiety, or lack of money, to a large extent we can't control the outer environment for very long. All physical forms eventually erode. How can you experience a sense of freedom and wholeness without the attachments to outer conditions? The solution is to let go moment by moment without attachments to outcomes, and you achieve this by knowing and trusting yourself, just like the idiot who is dancing unattached to anything other than feeling free and fully present with the moment.

Letting Go

I was having a conversation with my wife Edith while driving in the beautiful mountainous region of Western North Carolina. It was a magnificent sunny day with scenery that was as perfect as the weather. I was discussing the book I am writing (this book) and was explaining the benefits of understanding your personality profile. I had never really spoke of the subject at any great lengths with her before and did not know of her beliefs around personality type theories. I had a good idea of her personality type preferences, but never felt the need to express those insights. We are newly married and still learning about each other. I was explaining the benefits of understanding yourself and others through the personality profiling when she exclaimed in her Spanish accent: "I think all of that personality stuff is bullshit! I can do everything I want to do through God! No personality type indicator is going to tell me what I can and cannot achieve. I can become and do whatever I want to do, as long as I believe in the power of God! Jesus is my answer!"

Besides thinking, God! "Who have I married?" I was also interested in why she felt that way? Why she believed that the only answer is Jesus, and that there are no theories other than a deep belief in God and everything else is, in her words, "bullshit"? By not attaching to the outcome of the conversation and needing to be right, it was an opportunity for me to understand why my wife believes what she believes? Not having to be right and relinquishing control to the moment created more space within myself. The attitude of remaining open created less friction, and a greater sense of wholeness. It occurred to me that wholeness and freedom are the same; that wholeness is freedom! People who need to be RIGHT are rarely happy, because they are constantly looking for ways to escape their own inner entrapments and the need to feel in control. Often, this attitude will lead to various forms of addictions to escape their own imprisoned mind. Knowing yourself through a greater understanding of your personality type, along with understanding inherited patterns from the past, is the beginning of self-acceptance and purposeful living. In the next chapter, I will discuss what impedes self-acceptance and a greater appreciation for our life's journey.

Action Steps:

Talk to your camera or journal.

1. Take the MBTI indicator to assess your personality type
2. Write or discuss with your camera (See Camera Talk, chapter 7) three patterns that you bring into relationships.
3. When an opportunity presents itself, practice letting go moment-by-moment, releasing yourself from any agenda, or need to be right.

The New Selfish

The Man In The Glass

When you get what you want in your struggle for self
And the World makes you King for a day
Just go to the Mirror and look at yourself
And see what THAT man has to say

For it isn't your Father, or Mother or Wife
Whose judgments upon you must pass
The fellow whose verdict counts most in your life
Is the ONE staring back from the glass!
Some people may think you're a straight shooting chum,
And call you a wonderful guy,
But the man in the glass says you're only a bum,
If you can't look him straight in the eye

He's the fellow to please, never mind all the rest,
For he's with you clear to the END,
And you've passed your most dangerous, difficult test,
If the guy in the glass is your friend!
You may fool the whole world down the pathway of years,
And get pats on the back as you pass,
But your final reward will be heartaches and tears,
If you've cheated the man in the glass!

CHAPTER 3

> "We can never attain peace in the outer world until we make peace with ourselves."
>
> *Dalai Lama*

Self-Acceptance

If you don't take time to know yourself and process feelings, you will either adopt avoidance behaviors, such as social media, TV, smoking, drugs, alcohol, sex, or whatever addictions, or the suppressed energy will express itself as a mental or physical illness. Nature has a way of waking us up! I received such a wake up call on my 50th birthday.

Don't Panic

I was visiting a small town named Cardiff, close to San Diego, California, to celebrate my 50th with my girlfriend, who had scheduled a surprise trip, a part of which was to visit Hollywood and see the walk of fame. I had always fancied myself as an actor,

The New Selfish

and had dabbled in the craft over the years, but never committed, prioritizing money over my truer desires. On the drive out of town, we stopped at a coffee shop. After downing my second cappuccino, an eerie feeling washed over me. My heart was beating so fast that I could barely breathe? My girlfriend rushed over to the waitress. "We need an ambulance, now!" She informed her of a hospital located minutes from the coffee shop, and it would be quicker to drive. My girlfriend pulled me from my seat and beckoned me to run to the car. Gulping for air, terrified and afraid, I was taking my last breath; that I was dying! And on my birthday! Stupid thoughts ran through my mind; I hadn't left my condo to anybody? Who would pay my bills? "Are you crazy? What are you thinking about that for? You're dying". We were driving at high speed now, weaving in and out of traffic. Each moment could be my last. We came to a screeching halt outside the emergency entrance.

Still breathing, they guided me into a wheelchair and wheeled me to a room where a doctor administered a calming medication. My girlfriend left my bedside to make a phone call. I remember feeling terribly alone. The nurse hooked me up to an EKG, doing her best to calm me as the medicine took its effect. Thank God for drugs! I breathed a breath that had never felt so good. The doctor appeared. "Mr. Cavill, we checked your vitals. Everything seems to be fine. You've had a panic attack." "What! You mean none of that was real?" I noticed his nametag: Dr. Love? I'm sure people had commented on his name, and that I was likely not the first to do so. Still, it was my birthday! Dr. Love had showed up for me on my 50th birthday! How cool is that? I am special! I am loved! Thank you God! I was feeling so joyful! What a story! There's a message in here somewhere, is what I was thinking.

The New Selfish

And there was, which is why I'm sharing this with you. Dr. Love explained that panic attacks are real; that I had every reason to feel afraid. I cried like a baby. He said he normally didn't work at the Encinitas hospital and was transferred that day, as they were short staffed. Dr. Love had showed up just for me!

We left the hospital, filled a prescription at the local pharmacy, and went on our way. It was such a beautiful day, and as it was my birthday, we continued with our trip, celebrate new life, and visit Hollywood after all. I downed a couple of pills the good doctor had prescribed and relaxed. I was going to enjoy the rest of the journey, which is a wonderful metaphor for life. On the drive to LA, we stopped off at La Jolla beach, where I swam in the ice-cold waters of the Pacific Ocean, swimming far out to sea, floating on my back, looking dreamily at the clear blue sky, breathing in the life I thought I had lost, so very glad to be alive.

When we arrived in Hollywood, the walk of fame disappointed me and what a dump the place was. It was nothing like I'd imagined and so we agreed to leave early the next morning and make our way back to Cardiff and revisit the café where I had the panic attack to take in the experience more fully. And this is when I realized that energy does indeed drive our experiences, and that miracles happen every day! We have to learn to let go to receive miracles in our life. If we don't let go voluntarily, then the energy will show up to force us to let go. And likely, will show up as a wake up call, or worse. The name of the café, unbeknownst to me the day before, was the Pannikin restaurant! I had a panic attack at the Pannikin restaurant on my 50th birthday, where I visited the Scripps hospital, and was treated by Dr. love. This occurred while I was on my way to Hollywood, where so many marvelous stories are told. I could not have written a better script than that!

There are other stories within these writings that I think most people would consider as unusual examples of how our energy drives our life. When we suppress energy, it shows up in someway or another, to wake us up. If you wait too long, it will wake you up, and you may die. The body and the psyche can only handle so much suppression before it breaks down permanently. I had another similar experience, which was more difficult 10 years later on my 60th birthday with an Ayahuasca journey in Costa Rica where I experienced death. I share the story in Chapter 8, "The Inward Journey Part 2".

The occurrences in our life are reflecting to each of us our state of awareness. If you think you know a lot, you most likely do not. Life will teach you humility. Best to surrender now, or endure inevitable pain and suffering. My panic attack was a wake up call to pay more attention to my feelings and accept myself as imperfect, but still lovable and real, which is far easier to accept than being rigid and pretending to be perfect, which was my way of staying separate. If you want to avoid panic attacks, heart attacks, and other serious outcomes, then best to embrace your story as a teaching tool to free yourself and others. Pain is often a wake up call to a deaf world. Surrender now, or surrender later. Sooner is better, but later is better than never! What then impedes our self-acceptance? And what can we do to overcome the obstacles we face in changing patterns from the past so we may avoid potential trauma?

Judgment

If we continue to hold judgments around our behaviors, body image, money, relationships, and whatever other negative beliefs we unconsciously hold, then this energy only serves to keep us stuck, eventually making us sick, because it's resistance. What we resist persists! The programming from our limiting beliefs locks us into a gravitational holding pattern where we continue to experience the same or similar outcomes; the only change we will experience is an aging face reflected to us in the mirror. Stinking thinking and negative feelings perpetuate on themselves to create a personality based on past beliefs that we mostly inherited. It's not really who we are, but who we have thought and felt ourselves into being. We are birthing ourselves moment by moment from a past lineage that is not truly who we are. Staying safe is often an illusion that prohibits our truest desires to express our unique essence and authenticity to live a life of purpose. Our energy attracts our experiences, and that by continually holding on to judgments will keep us in the same toxic energy field destined to create the same energetic patterns in different forms. Self-acceptance is letting go of the constructs of who you think you are supposed to be, and giving birth moment by moment to who you are becoming by surrendering to the present moment. By releasing yourself from the need to be approved of, you will finally be free to express yourself without attachments to outcomes. It's in the letting go of the outcomes of what you think you wanted, that you then attract abundance into your life. It's a space thing, or a GOD thing, if you like.

Trusting in the enfoldment of your life is one of the most challenging obstacles to overcome. By giving space to the process without judgment or resistance, the energy field is free to attract what you need, not necessarily what you thought you wanted. As long as we are keeping resistance and judgment in our life, the likelihood is that similar circumstances will arise to confirm deep-seated beliefs from the past. These erroneous beliefs inevitably keep us stuck in the same energy cycle. The cycle of the mind going around and around, repeating the same thoughts over and over (unconsciously) does not differ from a hamster in a cage on his treadmill. Without having a clear perspective of the patterns of our behavior and accepting what is, there is no space for the pattern to change, and no escape from our self-imposed prison.

It is your story that can awaken you, providing you interpret the messages correctly. We are writing our story moment by moment. The path to self-acceptance is not a linear experience, but more an adventure into unknown and difficult terrain with many detours. The challenges of our journey reveal our current state of self-awareness. By reflecting on our behaviors, attitudes and reactions to challenging circumstances, we can honestly assess, without judgment, what we need to change and improve for a happier and more fulfilled life. Our evolution and the ensuing changes are necessary for each of us to transcend old patterns. These changes are challenging, but necessary. And so it is with every human endeavor worth undertaking. It is through the struggle that we learn to surrender and embrace our spiritual nature. It is not supposed to be easy! Just like a plant, we grow from the shit!

Beating Yourself Up

One early morning around 4 o'clock, I jumped out of bed and punched myself on my chest and jaw, knocking me to the floor! I couldn't stop from hitting myself! I was so angry for all the dumb decisions I'd made in my life that had brought me to the place of complete frustration. This negative energy must've been building in me for years. One morning, it released itself in a rage. I woke up that morning with the realization that I had no one to blame but myself. For the first time I really understood what it meant to beat the "shit" out of somebody, except the somebody was me! I was so angry with myself that the pent-up energy resulted in self-abuse, literally wanting to beat the shitty decisions out of me for all the mistakes I'd made. This is obviously not a good example of self-acceptance! This is an insane behavior and one I'm glad to say I've never repeated since. It's not that I have not made many mistakes in these past years since those occurrences, but what I've realized is that the world can be hard enough, and can, and will beat you up. We don't have to do it to ourselves. Unfortunately, we do, and everyone suffers. By learning to have compassion and empathy for myself, I can appreciate that life is a journey with an endpoint; no matter what the outside appearances may be, and whatever material things I may or may not gather. My life is a journey and I am writing the story, and so it is with you. The reality is no matter how much we may accumulate in the physical world, we are taking nothing in physical form with us. We are on a learning path where it's inevitable we will make mistakes. You're not supposed to be perfect. However, you are supposed to be fully and authentically you.

Guilt

I was reading an article in psychology today explaining that guilt can help a person overcome feelings of wrongdoing by deciding to make up for their misdeeds by helping others. This helps the wrongdoer to relieve their feelings of guilt and provides a better sense of himself as a giving person. Why I think this attitude can work, I feel we no longer need the initial step of feeling guilty. Personally, I think guilt is a useless emotion. First, when you feel guilty, it's a feeling of suppression and judgment about yourself that you are a bad person. You may have inappropriate behaviors, but that doesn't make you a rotten person. So much of organized religion is based on preaching guilt, which is a way of controlling. That way of controlling through guilty associations to ourselves may have worked in the past, but it's not doing a good job now, because we have so much information available to us to validate what's true and what is not. We can learn to trust in our own intelligence and measure our behaviors without having to go on a guilt trip. Cause and effect can be an excellent guiding system, not feelings of guilt! "The New Selfish" is an attitude where we focus on aligning ourselves with our true identity, which is love, by doing what we do because we like and love our self as that person. We understand that what we do to another we are doing to ourselves, because we are all one. We realize we cannot serve others effectively if we're harboring guilt. Our energy will not be pure because of the attachments and need for approval. Why? When you feel guilty, the energy creates a sense of not being enough, that there is something wrong with you. This is the feeling that guilt produces. Therefore, you can't be the giver you enjoy being because you're looking outside of yourself to gain approval, because inside, you don't feel enough. By recognizing behaviors are manifested through our awareness, we can forgive ourselves, and vow to use experiences to free our self and serve others. This is one reason the 12-step program works in AA and for other addictions. Guilt is an addiction that can be transformed with understanding, forgiveness, and creativity. By developing our gifts and sharing, we discover more of who we are, and are less likely to do harm to others as we embrace our story. We recognize the oneness of all life and our part in it. When you feel guilty, or you make another person guilty, you create separation. None of the above means that there should not be consequences for unacceptable behavior, as the Norwegian prison system suggests. We are far more effective in focusing on education and rehabilitation, which encourages self-acceptance and forgiveness. Guilt is not the answer! Guilt blocks self-love and acceptance of who we really are.

Norwegian Prison System

As of 2014, Norway's incarceration rate was 75 out of 100,000 people, as opposed to 639 inmates per 100,000 people in the US. In addition, since developing its new prison system in the 1990s, its recidivism rate has decreased from around 60-70% to only 20% as opposed to 76.6% in the United States! The main reason for these impressive statistics is because of a focus on "restorative justice," an approach that identifies prisons in the same category as rehabilitation facilities, rather than focusing on the punishment and mistreatment of its prisoners. Norway has the primary goal of reintegrating its prisoners as stable contributors to communities. The first way it is accomplishing this is by creating jail cells that closely resemble small dorm rooms. Many prisons in Norway have completely banned bars in their architectural design and have "open" style cells. At the maximum-security Halden prison, each prisoner has a toilet, shower, fridge and TV with access to kitchens and common areas.

Along with its innovative architectural style, Norway's prison system ensures that it provides a multitude of programs and courses

The New Selfish

that one could find at traditional recreational centers. The Halden maximum facility allows its prisoners to enroll in exercise classes as well as being able to learn woodworking and other activities. These programs ensure jails create a peaceful atmosphere, rather than a place for hatred and violence. Norwegian jails highlight the importance of education. Its primary goal is to encourage prisoners to not simply survive, but to live a full life once their sentence time reaches completion. Norway has banned life sentences, and one inmate at the Halden facility named Fredrik is serving 15 years for committing murder. In a 2019 interview, Fredrik opened up about his time at the prison and his accomplishments since starting his sentence. He is currently publishing a prison cookbook, received a diploma in graphic design, aced multiple exams, currently studying physics and hopes to pursue higher education once his sentence reaches completion.

At another facility, prisoners spoke of the impact of educational programs had on their mental health and hopes for the future. They admitted they had felt a sense of hopelessness because they believed the only actual skill they held was selling drugs. However, after taking several courses, they felt accomplished and realized they could master different skills. Now, through their time in prison, they have gained valuable skills that can assist them in obtaining legal jobs and a contributing member of society. They did not achieve these accomplishments by making the individual feel guilty, but more by understanding through effective rehabilitation that they are human and can be a valuable asset to society. The Norwegian prison system has recognized that guilt and judgment are not the answers if we want to free ourselves from destructive behaviors. Much the same as a wounded animal, we respond best to love, kindness, and understanding. Stronger measures and the issuance of capital punishment in any form should be a last resort. We are all wounded from a past that we had no control over. Some of us were more fortunate than others to the degree that we experienced suffering as a child. Unfortunately, we have a tendency to judge and make others guilty quickly because of our own ego and the need to feel righteous. Understanding and forgiveness can help to heal past wounds as we ourselves learn to be more congruent with each other and what feels right for us. The next time you experience guilt, whether you are the giver or receiver, remember that you are a work in progress; practice self-awareness to release yourself from the root cause of the feeling. Ask yourself what am I learning, and how do I let go? Remember, misery stems from focusing on yourself. Find ways to help others with compassion and love.

Failure

When we fail to achieve our goals and expectations, we can either learn from the experience, accepting the part we played, or are the victim. The latter only serves to keep us stuck because of the blocked energy living within our judgment. However, if we should decide to own our part in whatever the details might have been (which is probably the biggest obstacle to overcome) we can finally truly breathe and let go. We can only practice daily by letting go whenever the opportunity arises, remembering we are in the business of FREEING OURSELVES. We all experience failure in our lives, whether a broken relationship, failed business venture, financial choices that go wrong, or a general lack of self-discipline to achieve a goal; at some point or another, we will fail at something. Any life that is worth living will experience

The New Selfish

failure in one form or another. In fact, failure is predominant in our society where 65% of businesses fail within 10 years, and 50% of marriages fail; out of those percentages, who knows who is truly successful in the genuine sense of the word? How many people stay together just for the kids, or how many businesses are barely making it week in and week out? Most people will tell you that the biggest lessons in their life were from their failures, not from their successes. Let's look at what the experience of failure really does, and how it helps us to learn and grow, as well as teaching us humility.

I'm writing this book at a time having invested in a business venture, which to this point is not profitable and has been a constant drain on my finances and the inevitable emotional toll as it shows signs of potential success, which gives me hope, and then ensuing disappointment, which lets me back down. I've been on this roller coaster now for four years. Because I have a large investment, it's challenging for me to accept the situation. Basically, I'm stuck in judgment about the entire story and pissed that it's not working out…. YET! What is actually happening in the bigger picture is my ego is being ground down. I'm being forced to surrender, which is humbling. Michael Singer, author of the "Surrender Experiment" says that the greatest spiritual experience we can have is that of surrendering to what is. As the feeling of failure holds me in its grip, the diminishment of my ego forces me to surrender to something greater than myself. After all, I'm obviously not as brilliant as I thought I was. I fucked up! I need help! And so I surrender myself, which is where FREEDOM begins. By giving myself over to something greater than the small me that wants to feel important and superior, I take a more sincere interest in other people. I realize when I take a sincere interest in others; I'm escaping from my thinking mind, which left untethered can drive me nuts! Taking an interest in others frees me from the "Rat Race" that can be my thinking mind. As I'm aging, I feel connected to what is really important. I realize there is an end point to this journey, and by that recognition, I can put things into perspective. Sometimes you have to say, "fuck it!" not because you don't care, but because it's not worth it.

By writing this book, performing poetry or talking to my camera, I can stay focused and balanced by aligning myself with what feels true for me. If I was not engaged in these activities, I would be constantly going around and around in my head, creating more anxiety and frustration, which I often do when I'm not being creative. The reality is we only have so much control over outside influences what will and will not be. When we align with the energy of surrendering to "what is" it is easier to appreciate the here and now and be at peace. I'm not saying that failure is necessarily a good thing. I am saying failure is inevitable. If we can understand the process, then we can find gifts in all of our experiences, including all supposed failures. I'm working on this as I write these words. Like I have said frequently, we teach what we ourselves most need to learn!

Victim Mentality

If circumstances don't materialize in our favor, it's easier to adopt a victim mentality as opposed to taking responsibility for the outcomes in our life. If we do not surrender ourselves to a higher power during difficult times, then we may surrender to feeling sorry for ourselves and develop a victim mentality, blaming others for our failures, which is why as people age they can become bitter towards life. They cannot see a future as less time is in front of them, and the cold realization that their life may be a sad reflection of what they feared; that they are not special, not lovable, not good enough, and just another sad story. This is a sad and frequent occurrence for many people. The reality is we may have done everything right, and yet life still doesn't go our way. This is called experience. No one said this journey is easy. However, if you take each experience and learn from the outcomes, then you will discover it is your energy that has attracted the results. Results, if seen properly, will guide you to use your experiences as stepping-stones to greater awareness and future success, freeing you from the inherited lies that say you are not enough. Failing then can have redeeming qualities if seen from a wider perspective. It really depends on how you decide to accept the experience. When we are seeking success, there is an attachment to the outcome and what it should look like. We have a pre-ordained script in our head on how it should all go. If you've lived enough life already, you know that life doesn't always show up the way you would like it. Your character is revealed to yourself and others through challenging times. If we can stay present within the struggle, then we can grow beyond the circumstance. This is what personal growth is all about! If you can stay with the process, recognize that you are on a journey, that each supposed failure is the heavy lifting that is creating the muscles for your personal development, and grow beyond the old self, you can avoid the trap of identifying with a victim mentality. By relinquishing attachments to outcomes, and instead marrying the process by applying yourself fully to each step of the journey, you will naturally be authentic and show up as your true self as you learn to let go of past mistakes, recognizing each experience was a teaching tool to grow beyond the old self. We learn that failure is nothing more than a pathway to authenticity and genuine success. And we finally understand "it is done unto you, as you believe".

The Voice

We all know that there is a voice in our head that's continually talking! It's a constant never ending rap that can send us into our own hell. We process between 60,000 to 80,000 thoughts each day, 95% of which are unconscious, and the same thoughts as the day before. If we are programming ourselves every day, fueled by the unconscious thoughts from the day before, then it is probably in our best interest to notice what those thoughts are! It's also in our best interest to make the voice in your head your friend. However, making friends with an irrational person, in this case yourself can be challenging, as I'm sure some of you already know! If our thoughts are not coming from a place of compassion and love, then we can be pretty sure our thoughts are coming from ego, which is programmed to protect us from past patterns. Most of what we fear is not real, but imagined. I advocate "Camera Talk", journaling, writing, meditation, breath work, and plant medicines that can help release toxic patterns to increase self-awareness. We don't know what we don't know, until we expose ourselves to the light, similar to the old days of photography, where the developer dipped the negatives into a solution, prior to exposing the negative to a light, revealing the picture. We must expose ourselves to the light and transform negativity to see our self clearly, and speak the truth to ourselves by making the voice in our head our friend.

Irrelevant Lies

In my past, I have expanded upon the truth because I didn't feel good about myself. The programming from childhood said I wasn't worthy, and so I expanded upon the truth to feel good, because I didn't. Most people don't really care about your life; what they really care about is their own. And so, "white lies" are being told because of low self worth. While sitting in a restaurant bar, a stranger inquired where I lived? I shared I resided in a house on 6th Avenue in Saint Petersburg. What I didn't tell him was I renting a one-bedroom apartment, and rather inferred that I was living in a house that I owned. I was living in a house. However, the house comprised of four one-bedroom apartments, and I didn't own it. Previously, I had lived in a fancy waterfront condo, which I'd recently sold. I was used to living the "good life" and had to take some steps down because of a business failure. Now why do I bring up such an insignificant story? If you want to know people, pay close attention to the little things they say or do. It's the energy, not the details. I wanted to feel good about myself, and so inferred an untruth to a stranger whom I would probably never see again. What does that say about who I was being at the time? The important thing to remember here is not to judge, but to recognize patterns. When I arrived home that night (to my one-bedroom rented apartment) I said to myself, "Wow! You're still doing it!" I was aware of my behavior and the need to feel special because I didn't. The next time a similar situation arose, which it did, I would do it differently, and not expand upon a truth, or tell an insignificant lie to feel good. I would feel good from that moment forward by having integrity with myself, that I would honor what I am suggesting in this book, that I do all things because I like and respect myself as that person. The next time the conversation came about regarding where I lived, I was in the same restaurant talking to a different group of people. On this occasion, I spoke the truth that I lived in a rented one-bedroom apartment on 6th Ave. I felt free in that moment; thinking, no one really cares. The truth does set us free! It may be difficult, and it may piss you off, but it will set you free! I have learned that I respect myself, and I'm sure that it's true for you too, when I don't hide, or pretend to be someone I'm not. We don't have to share everything about ourselves with a stranger, but we certainly don't have to tell "white lies" to feel good. I like myself when I'm being me, not some fake edition to gain approval. We can embrace our story, not hide from it.

Expression or Depression

When we are habitually stuck in a survivorship mentality (very often conditioned from childhood), which is how our unconscious mind thinks to keep us safe, we store negative energy in our memory, which becomes an automatic response. Eventually, this suppressed energy has to express itself, or it will inwardly kill us emotionally or physically, either through depression, accidents, illness or disease, which is the reason I had a panic attack. We are consumers where thoughts become things; no different from the food we eat, which become who we are physically. And so it is with our thinking. We become our thoughts. That is why expressing our self through creativity is so important to wellbeing. Through expression, we can transform negative energy patterns, releasing suppressed energy through our emotions. We can become the alchemist, turning "lead into gold", and the old into new. By discovering the truth that lies dormant within us and expressing ourselves, we become renewed. As we learn to connect through our unique expression, we become at one with whom we are. Self-discovery and expression is a healthy path to self-acceptance, as the examples below show.

Comedian Brad Williams, who is 4' 4" tall, makes a great living through his own personal expression by making fun of his circumstances and how people treat him because of his size. He's hilarious! Brad transforms into what most of us would consider a debilitating circumstance by sharing his comedy routines through his experiences in everyday life. Another amazing example of overcoming debilitating circumstances is Nicholas Vujicic. Nick is a motivational speaker with no arms or legs! And yet he motivates "normal" people to overcome their challenges! There are many other examples of people with incredibly difficult circumstances that have overcome massive obstacles through their unique forms of expression. We cannot afford to allow ourselves weak excuses to stay stuck in our limited mind. Along our path, we must find healthy ways to express ourselves. So you may, or may not be a comedian, actor, dancer, speaker, poet, painter, or whatever art forms are creative gifts in our society. But there are unique gifts within you that you can develop and share. And likely you have an awareness inside that knows what they are. You must start from where you are, and at whatever stage of life you are at. By taking the journey inward and persisting with nurturing your gifts, no matter what level of accomplishment you may achieve, you are creating a relationship within yourself that gives you freedom to experience the NOW without attachments and judgment. We must nurture ourselves as if nurturing a child, remembering to laugh often with ourselves as we learn and grow. As we gain self-awareness and recognize we are at choice in how we decide to view situations and circumstances, that what we are doing in our lives, we are doing for ourselves because we love our self as that person; not because of a need to please, or to gain approval, is when we live authentically and express ourselves freely without self-judgment. If you continually seek acceptance outside of yourself, you will never trust in your own intelligence. By holding on rigidly to what we think we know, we will never allow ourselves to feel truly free. In order to let go, we must embrace the past that has brought us to this point in our lives. What can I do with what I have learned? How can I transform my story into something I am proud of? Who do I want to become in the process? These are good questions to help motivate us to become more self aware, and be happier and more purposeful.

Emotions

If it were easy to make change, then we would all do it. The challenge, of course, is to master our emotions so we can enjoy more peace, happiness, and a sense of purpose. Overcoming the thinking mind and the ensuing negativity, as Eckert Tolle discusses in his books, "The Power of Now" and "A New Earth" are the biggest obstacles to overcome. We are, in this respect, our own worst enemy. I find myself stuck in my head constantly thinking of the future and things that I must do. It's a source of anxiety that I have struggled with my entire life. Because of these mental challenges, along with my experiences growing up as a child, I have spent time in meditation retreats, workshops, plant medicine ceremonies, and other programs seeking to understand myself and quiet my mind. Much the same as working out our physical body, it's the same concept for our mind. Becoming self aware and practicing being present is a discipline and an art form that takes time. It's not a practice with an endpoint, but a constant realization of allowing ourselves to be present with what is now! Not in some future date when everything will be just fine when XYZ happens. We must embrace our past in order to move forward. We cannot continue to drag our old thinking with us and expect things will change. It's an art form to learn to let go without judging our self, or others. We cannot allow ourselves to be a victim to our own analytical mind, or to be a victim to past circumstances that we had no control over, other than to change our attitude. By seeking first to understand, practicing forgiveness and mastering our attitudes, we can nurture the truth within us that wants to set us free. By sharing these concepts through our demonstrations in the world, we can be reborn to a higher self, and use the past as reference points and teaching tools, remembering that we are teaching, often what we ourselves need to learn.

Self -Respect

When we align our thoughts, words, and deeds and deploy that energy as a navigation system for our life's path, we are more likely to feel good about who we are. Most of us understand that when we practice integrity, we respect ourselves. When we live by a code of ethics where our truth is of paramount importance, we feel good about whom we are. It is so much easier to look someone in the eye when you know you are aligning with your truth, and not some made up version to impress or deny. The biggest turn off to all of us is in-congruency; when a person says one thing and does another. So how do we overcome this negative energy, especially when often it's an unconscious habit? In order to become more self aware, we have to separate ourselves from our self, so that we can have an objective viewpoint as to what we do that is creating incongruence in our lives. That is why if you scan yourself at the end of each day and recognize your behaviors and attitudes, where you may have fallen from grace, you can become more aware of how you felt, and how you would like to feel in the future. It's important to do this without judgment, but merely as an observer, so you may practice a different attitude when a similar energy presents itself. I discuss this in greater detail in Chapter 5 "Attitude". If we appreciate we are a work in progress, and accept that we will make mistakes, and the mistakes are learning tools, then in time, we will be more effective and respect the person we have become.

Low Self-Esteem

People with low self-esteem don't value themselves, and therefore project feelings of inferiority onto others, especially those closest to them. The tendency is to project negative feelings because of their own frustrations. These are the same types that are slow to decide and quick to change their mind, because at the core level of their being they don't TRUST their own intelligence and don't value themselves. People with low self-worth want to feel good now, to escape the "cloud" that follows them wherever they go. This type of toxic thinking created a tremendous amount of suffering in my life. I was seeking short-term gratifications to put a Band-Aid on my wounds from childhood. If we truly valued ourselves, we would understand that there is a process to achieving anything worthwhile, and would commit to the steps necessary to achieve goals. In order for this to change, we must learn to nurture ourselves and give credit for the improvements as we make them. By paying attention to the results that you are creating, without judgment, you can then decide if you would like to try a different attitude the next time a similar circumstance reveals itself, which it inevitably will. By understanding we are a developing being, much the same as in technological advances such as the telephone, electricity, and what other advances have taken place in our world, we are also building on what has come before regarding our own awareness. We can learn to give ourselves a pat on the back when we have an "aha" moment as a realization of a pattern that has been keeping us stuck. Just as we are progressing with renewable energies to reduce toxicity in the environment, so it is with the powerful energy that wants to birth itself through us in our own personal evolution to release toxic patterns.

If we can only understand we are conduits for the energy that wants to free us to a new way of being in the world, then we are becoming part of the solution, instead of remaining part of the problem. It doesn't matter what age you are, you can learn to do things differently and enjoy a new way of BEING. As Gandhi said, "Live as if you were to die tomorrow, learn as if you were to live forever". By understanding you are writing your story, you can consciously partake in the chapters not yet written, and use the chapters that are. In the next chapter, we will discuss in more detail what impedes living authentically and what we can do to overcome obstacles to live a more happy and fulfilled life.

Action Steps:

Talk to your camera or journal.

1. What can you do with what you have learned? Brainstorm ideas that come to you. Commit to work on your best idea.

2. How can you transform your story into something valuable that you can be proud of? What do you need to do to give new meaning to your life?

3. Who do you want to become on your journey and why?

Being Creative

When I am creative, I am not frustrated
I'm in the moment NOW!
Not in some distant place, stressed out about the human race
I'm here right now, being my authentic self
I'm not thinking about health, wealth or anything else
I'm creating baby, and their ain't no maybe
I'm in the flow, oh yes I'm letting go!
And it feels so flipping good!

And guess what? It doesn't have to be angry!
Give it out! Give it out! That's what your soul wants to shout!
Come on, it's not about you
It's about all the souls you set free
When you become your own deity
Trust in you, what comes through you
Practice, whatever, if you have a few hiccups…
Or you feel you miss – don't worry about it
Your goal is to free you!

And guess what? When you do, people listen
That's when you know it's not about you
It's the gift that comes through you
When you surrender to what is…
To the truth that sets you free!

CHAPTER 4

"If one advances confidently in the direction of his dreams, and endeavors to live the life which he has imagined, he will meet with a success unexpected in common hours".

Henry David Thoreau

Living Authentically

If you're not living your life authentically, then you are in suffering. By trying to fit in with what you think is acceptable to others, or thinking about what you are going to get, it's likely you are not living authentically and in alignment with your true self. I'm not saying that you should not care what others think. I am saying it is more important what you think. No one cares about you, like you do. It is important to recognize that we are all operating out of self-interest, regardless of whether we are aware of it? Therefore, the question arises: what is truly in your best self-interest? When invested in other's approval, or thinking of what we are going to get, we lose our authenticity and are not valuing ourselves because of seeking fulfillment outside of ourselves, instead of nurturing the truth that wants to free us. We must bring ourselves fully to the moment and trust in the process that unfolds, learning to believe in our own intelligence as we develop our gifts.

For those who suffer with low self-esteem, we are in some manner performing, trying to be someone we are not, an actor seeking applause. When you walk off the "stage", you still go home with you. It should be of no surprise then that many of us become addicts through multiple forms of avoidance. Instead of naming them addictions, we should call them what they really are: illusions, or disappearing's. We finally surrender to live our life authentically and on purpose when we come to a place where, no matter what we do, we know something's missing. Whatever the avoidance behavior may be there is an increased awareness that something is amiss in our lives. By realizing that whatever we do to satisfy us in the outside world, we realize there are no places to hide, and nowhere to go. This is the turning point when we decide to let go of addictions, surrendering to a higher calling, and do the work. We conclude that the only way is to work through our doubts, fears, and insecurities by understanding that avoidance behaviors are only prolonging the inevitable effort we must make if we are to feel a sense of wholeness. By taking responsibility for our life's enfoldment, and practicing self-awareness, we can share our gifts, overcome our past-inherited fears, and give of ourselves without attachments to outcomes. We are not doing what we do for kudos, but for our own salvation, and we do it through authentic ways of giving.

And so we begin the journey to freedom by building an authentic relationship with ourselves because there is no other sane choice. There cannot be two of you anymore. The voice and you become one as you cross the bridge from your head to your heart.

Developing Your Gifts

In this book, I talk a lot about developing your gifts. Why is this important? First, it's important to connect to your deeper self, and what wants to express itself through you. Whether you become a champion in your arena is not the point. By connecting to your Self, you are no longer stuck in your thinking head, but connecting to the expression that wants to come through you. It doesn't matter what level you achieve compared to others in the development of your gifts, but that you align with the energy that wants to express through you. Perhaps you are a person who likes to do pottery, or bake cakes, or play musical instruments, or write poetry, or act, or design clothing, or dancing, or writing, or the many activities that provides a sense of Self by being in the moment with that part of you that desires expression. There is an energy that wants to express through your creativity. Your soul knows no such thing as failure, death, or competition. Your soul desires expression to feel free from attachments. For me personally, I feel connected to my creative source when I'm writing, speaking, acting, or performing poetry, anything where time stands still. When expressing myself fully, I experience a feeling of wholeness, where time is no longer an obstacle to overcome. Each one of us has a unique gift that we can contribute to the world and free ourselves from a critical mind that often berates us for not being perfect. No matter what station or age of life, it's never too late to begin. You likely know, or have a good idea, of what you enjoy doing. How then do we develop our gift? Initially, your ambition should not equate to financial gain, but a desire to feel at one with yourself, to be fully in the moment. If it turns out to be financially beneficial, then great! By being present and doing what we love, the less we feel the need for acceptance from others and the more likely success will show up in our life. When you value yourself enough, you will naturally spend more time with that part of you that knows. That is why learning is remembering who you are. As you develop your innate talents, it's only natural to desire sharing your gifts with others. By giving, you are confirming the truth that needs expansion through you. This is what it means to do what you love. Love is the "answer" when expressed through your true nature, which is to give.

Short-Term Gratification

Have you ever met someone that talks a good game, looks great, seems to tick all the boxes, and yet there was something off about their character? There are a lot of talented actors in the world. If we truly pay attention, we can, over time, recognize authenticity over good acting. We can adversely misjudge a person's character for two reasons: first, thinking about what we are going to get? Second, being Mr. or Mrs. nice guy. In either case, there is a need to satisfy an emotional hole. Out of this emotional need, we make poor decisions to experience short-term gratification. In the bigger picture, it is what we are unconsciously asking for in order to wake up. When disconnected from our authentic self, it's not unusual to seek escape routes to feel good temporarily, which is when suffering occurs to teach us lessons, as my story below shows.

Charlie

I met with an investment advisor named Charlie, who came recommended by a friend. When I invested $100,000 in stock purchases, I was very specific about not gambling on options, or any investments that were at high risk. Unfortunately, he ignored my requests, and I lost it all. When I look back on my thinking, when writing the check, it was short term and greedy. My new investment advisor friend was a good actor. He asked me what I would do if I could double or triple my money? I explained I had always wanted a little cottage in the mountains, and pictured myself in North Carolina, surrounded by waterfalls and running rivers. I was not thinking clearly, motivated by what I was going to get, not paying attention to the details. Charlie played his role perfectly, asking all the right questions, presenting me with a perfect opportunity to dream of my escape. In that time of my life, I felt lost, and was not living a life of purpose, wanting to fill the emptiness inside, acting impulsively. I was needy, and he could smell it. It was an expensive lesson I've never forgotten. It showed me I was not valuing myself. On reflection, I was being "Mr. nice guy", not doing my research, or asking the right questions. Looking back, I could have invested a test amount to see the results before investing a larger amount of money. I wanted to feel good about myself, gain a quick result, and feel like the "Man", because I didn't. I was seeking short-term gratification and paid a heavy price.

The New Selfish

Five years later, coincidentally, and unexpectedly, I was sitting across from Charlie at a wedding ceremony in Florida. I never expected to see him again, as he had left the United States and was living in Switzerland. When I sat at my table with other wedding guests, much to my surprise, he was sitting directly across from me. My friend, a family member who was aware of the circumstances, nervously began nudging me, fearful I may cause a scene, putting a damper on the wedding ceremony, which, of course, I would never do! I had not let go of the hurt experienced by the financial loss and embarrassment, still feeling victimized. I leaned across the table and whispered: "I need to meet with you".

Two days later, we met at a Starbucks. Charlie was 10 years my junior, but looked old and sad. His face was ashen, his skin blotchy and worn. He looked like death. Still, briefly, I thought about placing my hands around his neck and squeezing. Knowing that this wasn't a solution, I asked if he would explain what his life had been like for the past five years? I wanted to at least learn from the $100,000 experience, upon which he ignored my question and began defending his actions. I became impatient and angry! My blood boiled, as he was reminding me of my stupidity. I again patiently asked if he would explain what his life had been like over the last five years? He began his story. He had lost his money, too, and was no longer a stockbroker having lost his license. He divorced and saw his son sporadically. His mother-in-law was murdered during a robbery, his father terminally ill. We sat in silence, the realization of his pain seeping through my anger and resentment.

I shared that if I thought it would help, I would give him my forgiveness; but as I was not Jesus Christ, what he needed was to forgive himself. As I uttered these words, he sobbed, tears of pain streaming down his mournful face, desperately needing his own forgiveness. We stood in Starbucks that day and hugged each other. Both of us were crying. For myself, it was partly out of compassion, and also because I would never see my money again! I had, however, learned my lesson and he his. I explain the process of how to avoid the short-term gratification trap in Chapter 6, Decision Making and Commitments. If you have a tendency to be impulsive, or you procrastinate with decision-making, I strongly recommend following the guidelines in chapter 6 before making important decisions.

Overcoming Yourself

We cannot live our life authentically if we are harboring anger and resentment. Toxic energy is so powerful that it literally takes us over when triggered by memories of what we think something means. In religious terminology, we know this energy as the "Devil". We become someone we are not, triggered by suppressed memories from the past. By recognizing we are developing from a survivorship mentality where we still have much to do in order to train the ego to follow that what will actually be a very noble task, the ego can become our own personal dragon slayer when it buys into the program and supports our journey to become open and present through self-awareness. By becoming more self aware, we naturally develop our inherent gifts, which are the very things we give away without attachment to outcomes. The ego learns to support your desires by allowing you to be present with what is at the moment. It no longer has an identity to only protect you, but to support the true love of sharing who you really are. By releasing our false sense of self-importance, we are more able to allow the life force to flow through us. This is where your freedom lies, by taking your place in the bigger picture. As you free yourself from your conditioned mind, it becomes natural to move toward your true destiny, which is to develop your gifts and share them with others. This is how to live an authentic, purposeful life. In order for this journey to unfold, it is necessary to gain a clear perspective on your life and your journey. Much the same as when you stand close to an oil painting, where all you can see are dabs of paint. However, once you step back and create distance between yourself and the piece of art, you can see the picture clearly. And so it is with your life. By creating space between yourself and "you" that is "programmed", you can see yourself more clearly. I discuss practices including "Camera Talk" to assist in knowing yourself in chapter 7, "The Inward Journey Part 1".

Your Ego is Short Sighted

The ego micro manages our life. It is constantly assessing what is a threat to our existence. The ego is like a watchdog waiting to defend or attack. Our personality can change at any moment to protect our perceived territory. The reticular activation system (RAS) is a network of neurons that helps filter out what we perceive as unnecessary information, and zero in on what we believe is important. Therefore, the RAS searches out evidence to confirm beliefs. If you are a wounded child, and most of us are, then you will seek what threatens you from your associations to the past. As we like nothing more than to be right, we will find evidence to support our beliefs. This is an unconscious pattern, as most people don't know what they believe! The RAS zeros in on

The New Selfish

what it focuses on, from an inherited belief system that we are unaware of! The ego's primary job is to keep you safe and search for evidence to protect you from outside danger. It validates its actions based on what you unconsciously believe as a potential threat from your belief system. The ego will then compound the evidence (however trivial the evidence may be) into a pattern of reactions that are often destructive. To the ego, it is merely doing its job, much the same as an attack dog protecting its master.

For example, if a dog has attacked or bitten someone, that individual is less likely to approach a dog, even if it is a golden retriever! It's not that they don't like dogs necessarily, but moreover they have a memory from the past, which perceives dogs as a threat. This activation system operates by seeking threats, whether a love partner having a harmless discussion with someone, a money issue, or whatever the circumstances may be that threatens the status quo. The ego's primary job is to keep you safe and search for evidence to protect you.

In keeping with the dog example, and a visual of how the ego can behave, I fed my two beautiful golden retriever dogs leftovers at a party I was hosting. As the party was ending, I fed the dogs leftovers of chicken breasts and gravy. They gulped down the feeding in seconds. Moments later, they threw up onto the kitchen floor. Much to the horror of my guests, my two beloveds gulped down what they had thrown up. Watching my two beautiful animals behave so repugnantly was both amazing and disturbing.

When you experience the same negative energy patterns, whether it be with a coworker, family member, life partner, or whoever else, where you continually throw back-and-forth the same stories, either inside of your own head, or verbally with each other, of why they are ruining your life, then you are stuck

The New Selfish

in the ego, and likely so are they. You are eating your own vomit, along with theirs. If that is not a visual image that will wake you up, I don't know what is! Even if you are a dog lover! The above example is a metaphor for how people behave when they are in the ego's grip, held in a destructive energetic pattern, recycling the same energy from the past. The energy that created the misery in the first place was never about the other person, but perceptions and beliefs from the past. To avoid negative behavior patterns we must train the ego to recognize what is a genuine threat and what is a pattern. Are we doing the same thing? Is it the same pattern, only with another person? Can we become more self aware as to our participation in reactions that only serves to keep us separate and unhappy? We do this by observation, not judgment. As the ego releases its addiction to unconscious behaviors, we no longer march to the beat of a distant drum. We are no longer the ant blindly marching to the beat of the past, but a human being-present with the truth that is who we really are. Your ego no longer judges you and others to keep you safe, but becomes an intelligent, albeit primordial observer trained with a greater perspective on what is real as opposed to what we imagine, based on facts, not erroneous fears from past conditioning. This is the wisdom card that expands as you learn to be your own unbiased observer. Your ego now knows its proper role, which is to support your unique expression so you can finally give without attachments, trusting the process.

Authentic Feedback

Ray Dalio built his business "Bridgewater" into the world's largest hedge fund on the foundation of what he calls "Idea meritocracy".

The New Selfish

His unparalleled success is based on the idea of absolute truth and "radical transparency". Ray has built a financial empire based on the premise that his people are free to express themselves without judgment, irrespective of where they are in the hierarchy of his company. Each employee is aware of their own thoughts and the thoughts of the other attendees in the company. By employing what he refers to as radical transparency, people can step back and have a clear perspective on what works and what doesn't. Rays employees are not judged for outlandish ideas or thoughts, but encouraged to speak openly. Ray discusses how this protocol works by using several examples in his company meetings. During these meetings, they provided all employees the same respect as high-level executives. New employees have written highly ineffective scores and comments when Ray himself has given presentations. Ray can look at everyone's opinions and scores on his effectiveness without personalizing the feedback. Each attendee views the comments and scores of each participant. Because all attendees view the information, each observer can recognize varying perspectives from the same presentation. By having transparency, without judgment, people can learn to open their minds to other perspectives and ways of thinking. Ray adopted this attitude both in business and in his personal life after making large-scale errors based on egoist decisions, and not on the information available to him earlier in his career. Because the lessons learned from his own admitted arrogant attitude led him to understand that flexibility and observation were more important than his previous need to be right.

Authentic Communication

When we look at an effective communicator, they align themselves (body), their message (mind), and their purpose (spirit). Effective communicators are congruent with their thoughts, their words, and their deeds. They don't have to think about body language, voice tonality and each word spoken based on effective communication statistics; they may have studied these communication skills, but are not self-consciously thinking about themselves when sharing their message. Effective leaders are at one with their message and we feel it. If the message they are sharing resonates wholly within them, then it rings true. Excellent communicators, such as Tony Robbins, Joel Osteen, and other leaders, have learned to connect to their own truth where they are standing on solid ground, aligned with their purpose. If you have had the good fortune to be present in Tony's seminars, you will know the power I am referring to. People that come from this deep place of integrity are congruent. Therefore, we naturally trust a person with such characteristics. There is also a strong sense that the message they are sharing is personal to each of us. They are master communicators who have practiced honing their gift and are present with their message. Their intention is to give, not to seek approval. They are in the sharing business, not the approval seeking business, where they have mastered their art, trust their own intelligence and are living on purpose.

Authentic Acts

If you know anything about acting, you will have heard the term "back story". The actor aligns himself with who he is portraying by immersing into the character's past. He can go within the persona of the character and gain a deeper understanding of whom he is playing. While in this process, he is not judging the good or bad traits, but seeking to feel his way through to the essence of the character and understand who he is, and how he became who he is, or was, and why? As you discover your own true self and accept your own back-story, without judgment, you naturally grow beyond the past. As we allow ourselves to release judgments and enjoy sharing from the present moment, the more the life force can flow through us. This clean energy cleanses us from the toxic past, where we no longer have to put on some act to be accepted. Our authenticity can speak through us without attachments to the results previously yearned for. The results naturally take care of themselves, no longer attached to the "Am I good enough" syndrome, and what other people may or may not think. We can finally allow ourselves to sing our song of truth, and not be concerned about others' approval, but how we feel, not with the intention of how we are affecting others, but how we feel in the moment with our message, practicing our expression, and discovering our own inner beauty.

When free from attachments to outcomes, you experience the feeling of atonement that is born from being present with your message through the unique expressions that only you can give. This is the ultimate loving of oneself! As you know yourself at a deeper, more intimate level, accepting your past as a learning tool, your desire to live authentically naturally takes precedence over seeking outside approval. In the next chapter, I discuss strategies on how to be aware of your attitudes to help overcome negative behavior patterns that can keep you stuck in toxic patterns.

Action Steps:

Talk to your camera or journal.

1. Ask yourself when you go into a reactive state how long do you want to stay in this place of reactivity? Is it really worth the price you're paying at the cost of your peace of mind? Be consistent with asking yourself, was it worth it? If you can catch yourself prior to reacting, ask yourself before you fire off any damaging comments or behaviors. Is it worth it? You may recognize negative emotional states are addictive, and that some part of you actually likes the feeling. As you recognize toxic patterns, without judgment, you can let go of the need to feel the rush of self-importance, which is a protection mechanism from the ego. Be diligent in the "Wisdom Game" and you will grow in your awareness and your effectiveness.

2. Be aware of addictive thinking and continuous thoughts about the future. Connecting to nature is a helpful way to be present, as well as connecting to your own breath.

3. Become aware of your need to complain. Don't judge any of your thoughts and behaviors. The object is to become aware of toxic patterns so you may decide what is working for you, and what is not. Remember, this is the "Wisdom Game". Play it fairly. The "Wisdom Game" is about aligning with what feels good and right for you by creating closeness. Be diligent and you will grow in your awareness and your effectiveness.

The Messenger

How long do I have to sit, to wait?
How long to be the messenger?
What fear is it?
What torment is it that keeps me from this holy place?
It is my mind that does not accept myself
That keeps me in this lonely space...
Sitting and waiting... And yet I hear...

Start from where you are
What is my initiation to leap this gap?
To transcend this space of nowhere
To see, to feel this destiny inside of me that screams...
Hear me!!! Show me my map, and I will follow as surely
As the day follows the night

The knight of armor, the knight of light
I will fight your fight! I surrender to your almighty might!
Speak to me! Use me for your sight!
I am and will be your guiding light
I only want to serve!

Oh really? Is that right?
Mighty words you proclaim
Are you sure you are not proclaiming some inner need for importance and personal fame?
We must take our temperature as we make such claim
What is your desire? What is your fear?
Are you in it for the glory?

The New Selfish

Is it important that people know your name?
You will fall short if you are imbued within this game

Your loves, your dreams will not appear
Some other force will bind you to your shame

To guide yourself between these two impostors
Free from right or left, unattached to this or that
To stand in your center, free from all the dark chat
To speak your truth with love for all
Attached to nothing but the passion of your call

Free at last, it will show up now!
The way, the path, no longer some distant how
The method, the means will find you
As you release to your transcendent vow
Moment by moment....

CHAPTER 5

> "Your thoughts and feelings come from your past memories. If you think and feel a certain way, you begin to create an attitude. An attitude is a cycle of short-term thoughts and feelings experienced over and over again. Attitudes are shortened states of being. If you string a series of attitudes together, you create a belief. Beliefs are more elongated states of being and tend to become subconscious. When you add beliefs together, you create a perception. Your perceptions have everything to do with the choices you make, the behaviors you exhibit, the relationships you chose, and the realities you create."
>
> *Joe Dispenza*

Attitude

Several years ago, I went on a date with a lady who has since become a dear friend. Prior to the date, we had gotten to know each other over a period of months, chatting on the phone and philosophizing. After dinner, she invited me back to her home for a glass of wine. Upon entering her apartment, I couldn't help but notice many framed pictures and various figurines of angels. Wherever I looked, there was an angel staring at me. She explained she had an intimate relationship with angels since she was a little girl. After a brief while, having had a few glasses of wine, she disappeared upstairs, where after a time she beckoned me to join her. As I made my way to the top of the landing, I noticed the bedroom door was slightly ajar. I could see the flickering of lights dancing from inside the doorway. Angels? Candles? What was I getting involved in now? I had once met a woman who had claimed her mother was a witch; she had shown me her Ouija dolls and the needles her mother used to punish her victims. Fucking hell! Is she another one, is what I was thinking! I opened the door and entered the bedroom. She was lying seductively across her bed, a flimsy negligee revealing her young, sultry body. It was the candles, however, that got my attention. They were everywhere! Blinding my eyes. They were on the windowsills, the furniture. "You don't have a sacrificial knife underneath your pillow, do you?" I said. I began searching under her pillow. "When's the plane landing? WTF Rosetta, what is this? Is this how you trap all your men?" She was laughing! She said, 'You've ruined the moment!' I said, "I'm sorry! I was blinded by the light!" We both laughed. I gave her a hug, blew out the candles, (which took a while) and turned to leave. She said: "Dave, Pay attention to your dreams tonight". I laughed! I had no clue what she was talking about? I never paid attention to my dreams. I arrived home and went to bed, not giving the suggestion a second thought.

Waking From The Dream

I was one of many, wandering in a wilderness, dressed in a white robe, carrying a large lump of smelly stuff, embracing its contents as if hugging myself. I was not aware of smell, or of anything. In a moment, I realized a spiritual presence standing beside me. I took a deep breath, as if it was my first. There was a presence within me I had not felt before. I slowly turned, not aware that I could see. I had been wandering for a very long time. And then I saw him! His radiant blue eyes engulfed me. I was he, and he was I. I was staring into the abyss of me. I felt only love. He was showing me, me. Surrendering, I let go. I felt free, unchained. I was free to be me! NO MORE FEAR! I was coming home! The weight drained from my shoulders. "David, you can put it down now", were the first words he spoke. Much like a child with his father, I wondered where I should put the smelly pile I'd been carrying for so long? "Where? Where should I put it?" I asked. He smiled into my eyes; I felt calm and peaceful. "There", he said. "You can put it down over there," pointing to a space where there were no other "walkers". I took a few steps and placed the large smelly lump on the ground. It felt as if I was seeing for the first time, breathing for the first time, and perhaps I really was? He said to me in a calm voice, "Follow me." We weaved our way through the throng of humanity, all aimlessly wandering in a deep sleep, dressed in white robes, as was I. I felt compassion as I made my way, because I knew their pain. I knew they were asleep, that the pain was their sleep. I knew because I was them- that they were me.

We came to a stone stairway and began ascending the heavily worn steps. I became aware that I was not the first to make this journey. The soles of many feet had been on these steps long before my ascension. As we walked the stairway, from my new vantage point, as far as my eyes could see, were souls walking aimlessly, embracing their own mass of smelly stuff. The landscape upon which they were sleepwalking was barren, rocks and dust, no vegetation. No life. Lost souls sleep walking in a desolate space of lifelessness. Humanities inner fear at its deepest root: Lost and abandoned. No wonder letting go is flipping hard! Is what I was thinking? We're all hanging on to our smelly stuff and think that's what love is! I turned towards my Guide and asked, "What about them?" pointing to the mass of white robes. "What about all of them"? He said, "Their time will come. When they are ready, they will come too". When we arrived at the top of the stairway, it was nighttime. I could see a large bonfire burning in the distance, silhouettes of souls dancing around its perimeter. I looked up towards the magnificent night sky, a sea of stars dancing in the blackness. He had left my side and was making His way back down the stairway. He turned and smiled a warm smile, pointing in the fire's direction. I danced with the dancing souls, feeling free for the first time.

I awoke, wiping tears from my eyes. Everything from the night before was so clear. I was finally awake. And then I began my day, and slowly over time, I drifted back to sleep.

You Are Unique

Deep inside of myself, I know I am special, that I am unique. And of course, this is true, as it is for you. There is no one quite like you, and there is no one quite like me. We may share similarities, but we are uniquely different. Without joining with something greater than ourselves, we will never experience our true uniqueness. We will not be extraordinary without connecting with the spiritual power that lies within. The words EXTRA - ORDINARY only means more of the same, unless the words connect to become EXTRAORDINARY. It is our nature to desire expression, a hunger deep inside calling us to join with our destiny. To be the truth of who we are, we must join with a higher power that wants to work through us as an expression of healing. The "dream" showed me I had to put down the smelly stuff from the past and follow my spiritual guide on the stairway to heaven. That awakening was not possible without surrendering to something greater than myself through understanding and forgiveness. By trusting in a higher power, we can embrace the past. Understanding the lessons was necessary for compassion and empathy to bring us to the present moment with greater awareness. We can learn to let go of negativity by applying new attitudes when our reactions are not in sync with who we truly are, and how we would like to feel. We can free ourselves from past patterns and practice doing things differently. When we fall from grace, as we inevitably will, and react poorly, our job is to be the barometer of what feels best and right. Your job is to become the observer of your behaviors overtime to be self-aware, so you may experience self-acceptance and love. It's a process that takes time as we grow to higher states of awareness.

Understanding Attitude

When I practiced hypnosis, I worked with various clients who wished to stop smoking. The clients 1 worked with were aware that smoking was dangerous and damaging to their health. People who smoke cigarettes know they should not smoke. They are fully aware of the dangers of smoking, of the impending potential for lung cancer and untimely death. And yet, they still smoke. Smoking cigarettes is an emotional reaction that transcends to our physiology. And so it is with a negative attitude. We've already discussed that 95% of our behavior is based on unconscious actions and thoughts the same as the ones from the day before. We do what we do mostly unconsciously, because we are creatures of habit. Smoking cigarettes and living with a negative attitude affect our mental and physical health. Negative attitudes and feelings of helplessness and hopelessness can create chronic stress, which upsets the body's hormonal balance, depletes the brains chemicals required for happiness, and damages the immune system. Chronic stress can actually decrease our lifespan. We develop habits such as smoking cigarettes and other addictions unconsciously to avoid feeling feelings. If a person who smokes cigarettes, or has a poor attitude towards life valued himself or herself, (and was consciously aware of what they were doing) they would quit the behavior. People with a negative attitude towards life are punishing themselves because, unconsciously, they don't believe they should feel good. They don't feel worthy! Addicted to a negative attitude, they unconsciously allow their mind and unconscious reactions to control their behaviors. Their negativity is their identity. As Joe Dispenza states, the body becomes the unconscious mind that they unintentionally feed. Eckert Tolle calls it the "pain body". And so they feed on pain, drama and depression, walking with a cloud above their head, like a rain magnet, attracting what they believe.

The Law Of Attraction

Lao Tzu, an ancient Chinese philosopher, once said: "Watch your thoughts, they become your words; watch your words, they become your actions; watch your actions, they become your habits; watch your habits, they become your character; watch your character, it becomes your destiny." We attract what we put out. This idea has clearly been around since ancient times, and many credit Buddha with first introducing this notion to the world. The "Secret" a 2006 self-help book written by Rhonda Byrne, is based on the belief of the law of attraction, which claims that thoughts can change a person's life. Across nearly all religious thought, and as testified by some of the greatest thinkers of our time, the law of attraction is the most powerful force in the universe. It's a law that began at the beginning of time that determines the order of things within the universe. It forms your life experience, and it does so through your thoughts. The book claims that all those who become wealthy have done so by using "The Secret" either consciously or unconsciously. As we think predominantly about wealth, for example, and don't let contradictory thoughts enter our mind, then wealth is created as we act on our beliefs. According to "The Secret," this then is the law of attraction in action. Napoleon Hill's book, "Think and Grow Rich", states that by repeating a set of daily mantras and reprogramming our thoughts, we can manifest great riches. Our current life reflects our past thoughts. You attract what you think about. To change your life you must change your thinking. You literally think your life into existence. What you are thinking now will create your future life. This is the theory of the law of attraction. One way to master your mind is to learn how to quiet it. Each teacher who contributed to "The Secret" practices daily meditation. By quieting our minds, we become aware of our thoughts, and thus learn that we can control both our thoughts and our life. The secret is to not dwell on the past with guilt, shame and judgment, but to realize it is the thinking that made it so, and focus our attention on the new life that awaits our presence.

Changing Attitudes

The deep-seated trust issues inherited from my past, accelerated and compounded upon by the laws of attraction, kept me "safe" and very much alone. I was unaware of this attitude and blocked abundance from entering my life. A negative attitude is an unconscious way of blocking receiving because of a lack of self-love. A negative attitude is an addiction, an addiction to feeling unlovable. We often justify our negativity so we can avoid showing up and consequently blame others for our unhappy life. People with negative attitudes have no way of comprehending they don't value themselves, because unconsciously, it's all they know. There have been times I have caught myself when laughing and thinking: "Wow! I can be happy". It's an unfamiliar feeling. And then the happy feeling goes away, like a magician clicking his fingers; I'm back to where I was. At a deeper level, I'm afraid to trust. The old heaviness slivers its way back in, back to what is familiar. Because of our ignorance, we are unaware that we are, in fact, co-creators with the universal energy that runs through each of us; we are pouring ourselves energetically into a mold. If we feel unworthy because of past conditioning, then we will fill the mold with negativity and live a life based out of those beliefs, of what is familiar. It becomes our identity. In order to free ourselves, we must forgive others and ourselves because of what we have attracted so far, based on our unconscious thinking and feeling. If you are one of those people, as I have been, who has suffered with a fearful view of life, then once you've read this chapter, you can practice a new awareness around attitude. You can move differently, learn differently, and live differently. We are not our past, and we no longer have to stay conditioned. By nurturing ourselves through conscious awareness, we can change our attitudes. We can learn to recognize then that attitudes can be a strategy. That we can have it, and it does not have to have us! We can free ourselves from our own imprisoned mind. When an emotion has us under its control, we are helpless to the reactions that dominate our lives. By acknowledging our attitudes, we can then use newfound awareness to change how we behave and feel. We can practice new attitudes and see how that feels compared to our previous experience with a similar circumstance. We can learn to play with our attitudes and discover what works best, instead of being enslaved to the same old reactivity.

Attitude Strategy - Influence

When we're living our lives authentically by consciously overcoming the many challenges that are part of our personal growth, our energy naturally resonates with others. We influence others by our actions because we are always teaching (consciously or not) through our demonstrations. Demonstrations are the manifestations of our attitudes in the outer world, mirrored for all to feel and see. As we become more aware, we are better able to influence others by being present without an agenda. When we are in the present moment, we are open, and others feel it.

feel a sense of trust when in our presence, because we are not stuck in our logical thinking survivorship mind of what's in it for me, or am I being approved of? The charisma of being present with another person is a gift that we give both to ourselves and to the other. When we are open to giving and receiving with no agenda, joining occurs as we become one with each other through TRUST. If we add a sense of humor and a light heart to the equation, then that is influence. Who doesn't like to be around a sincere, compassionate person who is wholly present and loves to laugh? Show me a person like that, and I will show you a successful person with influence and as many friends as they desire.

Attitude Strategy - Communication

When you practice compassionate and empathic communication, there is a feeling of oneness as you relate to the other as if they are another aspect of yourself. By being present in the moment, and unattached to outcomes, it is far more likely that you will create a deeper connection both within yourself and whomever you are communing with. We have spent our whole lives fitting into a society that measures success in old-fashioned materialistic ways that do not create a feeling of community. When you can live from a space where you feel connected to the flow of life, which is to trust, good things happen. We can best influence others by freeing ourselves through self-awareness, mastering our gifts, and purposefully living in the now. This is a process that takes a genuine commitment to heal the wounds from the past and live authentically. As you learn to let go of agendas and practice being present, energy patterns change and new opportunities arise. The

The New Selfish

process of self-discovery can be difficult, but also highly rewarding as you let go of the chains that have bound you. I've witnessed many people free themselves from past beliefs that kept them in their own prison. After they have wiped the snot and tears away, they very often look 10 years younger; such is the burden they have been carrying for so long. What is also interesting is how others feel more connected when we show vulnerability. As Brené Brown discusses in her books and pod casts, vulnerability is courageous and rewarded. When a person softens through self-honesty, we are more likely to feel compassion as we are all connected to the same source. Brené compares courage to being vulnerable as a soldier going into battle. The soldier courageously risks his life in service to others, which is the ultimate act of vulnerability. Ernest Hemingway famously stated in his novel "A Farewell to Arms", "A brave man dies only once, a coward dies a thousand deaths". Being open and honest can be scary but has many rewards, the greatest of which is the feeling of authenticity. A friend recently commented that I was sincere. I responded with, "what else is there?" If we can't be sincere, which is being vulnerable, what are we doing with our lives? None of this rhetoric means we can't have fun! Being real can be great fun! We can laugh about past mistakes, not hide from them. It feels good to be freed from self afflicted judgment, and the ensuing feelings of shame and guilt. We can use experiences as teaching tools, not from ego or shame, but from the perspective of what is and what was. Your story is always your story. Your attitude towards your story will change your life!

New Attitudes

At the end of each day, before sleep, scan your day. How did you do? Ask yourself what other attitude could have worked better in whatever circumstance you are reviewing? What other choices could you have made in the same circumstance? The next time a similar circumstance presents itself, try a new attitude and feel how that works? Notice that I use the word FEEL. When you lay your head on the pillow, go through the day and scan where you could have used a different attitude in whatever circumstance you are replaying in your mind. Play the scene over in your imagination and try out a different attitude. It could be as simple as when you were buying a cup of coffee at the coffee shop. Did you connect with the salesperson? Did you make eye contact? Did you take a moment to smile at a stranger? Or conversely, it could be the argument you had with your co-worker or spouse. The idea here is to become more aware of your attitudes. The next time a similar situation presents itself, remember to PRACTICE a new attitude and see how that feels. Before you go to sleep, scan your day. How did you do? No judgment, just more awareness!

Willingness

Sadhguru, the Indian mystic, discusses happiness as simply a decision about willingness. If you are deciding to do something, whatever the decision may be; you are more likely to experience peacefulness if you undertake the activity with an attitude of willingness, instead of resentment. If you can indoctrinate this as an attitude, you will naturally feel more at peace. It's obviously an attitude that needs practice. In practical terms for example, if you are the one in your household that is taking out the trash, and also cleaning the kitchen floor, and perhaps your spouse is not doing his fair share of the chores, then you may feel resentful as you are unhappily cleaning and blaming, at the same time. Conversely, you can be a willing participant while taking out the trash and cleaning the floor because you are choosing it. If you feel your spouse is not contributing, you can ask for help from a position of strength, not anger or neediness. If both of you understand the premise of whatever you're doing, you're doing for yourself, and are adopting an attitude of willingness towards life together, there is less likelihood to have conflict. Have them read this chapter!

Attitude of Gratitude

An attitude of gratitude is where we learn to appreciate the apparent small things in life. A person with an attitude of gratitude takes time to reflect on what they have, not what they do not. They are not constantly searching outside of themselves for happiness; only to discover that what they thought would make them happy does not. Grateful people train themselves to appreciate what most of us take for granted, either through natural optimism or by comparison to a tragedy or illness. They look at the sky, the ocean and all of nature's beauty and feel a genuine sense of appreciation. Having an attitude of gratitude is important because it shifts our focus from our own small self to a larger picture, providing us with a sense of wholeness. An attitude of gratitude means making a conscious habit to express thankfulness and appreciation in all areas of our lives. Having an attitude of gratitude means we operate from a place of abundance, rather than scarcity. When we develop an attitude of gratitude, we feel happier and more positive as the feeling of gratitude shifts our mindset. When we express gratitude, we naturally feel more positive and are more intentional. Developing an attitude of gratefulness requires us to shift our mindset and make it a daily habit to be thankful for everything we appreciate in life. As we develop a sense of feeling grateful, what we focus on expands, opening us to receive. The energy of gratitude is at the same vibrational level as the energy of receptivity. Being grateful improves our self-esteem and enhances our awareness of the present moment. When we feel grateful, we naturally feel more positive and are more present. As we learn to express gratitude daily, the things and people we appreciate grow in value. Adopting a grateful attitude assists us to see more things to be grateful for, which makes us happier, more content and appreciative. Being a positive, grateful person attracts other people into our life who have a similar mindset. As you practice forgiveness, recognizing past behaviors, and the behaviors of others were born out of ignorance, you can also practice gratitude, letting go of what no longer serves you. Be thankful for your story, all of it has brought to the place you now stand. In the next chapter, I share the importance of making Intelligent conscious decisions and commitments, and how to approach the process so you may save yourself unnecessary pain and suffering.

Action Steps:

Talk to your camera or journal.

1. At the end of each day, before sleep, scan your day. How did you do? Ask yourself what other attitude could have worked better in whatever circumstance you are reviewing? Play the scene over in your mind and try a different attitude using your imagination. Be creative! What other choices could you have made in the same circumstance?

2. The next time a similar circumstance presents itself, try a new attitude and feel how that works?

3. Practice gratitude. What you are grateful for and why? You can also speak to your camera to help connect to your deeper self.

The Man In The Tree

I was sat in a rocking chair, in a valley
Surrounded by mountains
I could hear the mountain stream flowing by
It was beautiful and serene
The stars were more than I had ever seen
Like a hundred thousand sparkling eyes smiling down at me
I felt connected, I felt free...

I looked to my left, (it was dark outside)
But I could see... a figure, an image, a man?
He was stuck in the tree!
I cold realization came over me
The man I could see in the tree...was me!

I was the man stuck in the tree
I was free here, but stuck there
I knew in my belly... that he was me
That I was the man stuck in the tree!
And then I knew... I had some work to do
That was me, and I was NOT free!

I got the message, and wondered...
How long would it be? Would I ever be free?
I spent a long time in the tree
Stuck in past fears, frozen in anxiety
It was many years ago that I received the message

The New Selfish

A lifetime to know what it is to be stuck and not to feel free
And yet I stayed stuck clinging to the branches of that tree
Afraid to let go and trust in me.

The truth is I love being me....
Who doesn't love being themself?

I stopped feeding the vines with my fears and anxiety
I use the memory of the tree now...Not only for myself
But for whomever else who would choose to be free
Where I can be there with my hand on their back
Never again to be in the grip of the Vine
Free at last, at home with the Divine
It was my attitude that shifted and set me free!

CHAPTER 6

"The biggest commitment you must keep is the commitment to yourself"

Neale Donald Walsch

Decision Making and Commitments

In this chapter, it's time to commit to the work needed to overcome past habits that may have kept you stuck in the same, or similar, energy patterns. We may define insanity as doing the same thing over and over and expecting a different result. Entering unknown territory can be scary and challenging. However, it is important to remember you are on a life journey with an endpoint. When you get to the end of your life, you want to know that you entered the arena, and showed courage, making commitments to be the best version of yourself. You may not have at first succeeded, but you didn't give up in your pursuit to be more. You let go of what no longer worked and

The New Selfish

embraced what did. You used everything that came before you as a teaching tool for others. You freed yourself from the past, and you did it despite your fear. You were not perfect, but you were authentic, and that is what you loved most about you. This and more can be your legacy if you honor yourself and make the right commitments. This chapter can save you a great deal of discomfort in your life if you are ready to listen? If not, then you will fall back in to the same or similar patterns, which means you're not ready. Pain is a megaphone to a deaf world. This chapter is when the rubber hits the road! Do you want to live a purposeful life? If you honestly are ready to say "that's enough!" and truly desire a deeper meaning to your life, then enjoy the process, suck it up when you have to, and do the work! Will you be afraid sometimes? Hell yes! However, when you make intelligent commitments, as explained in this chapter, belief in yourself will increase with each new experience. When you are clear with your intentions, it's far easier to follow through with your decisions and separate the "voice" in your head that says, "You're not good enough". Do as many of the exercises as possible listed at the end of this chapter either through journaling, or with "Camera Talk". You cannot overcome the old self if you are unaware of exactly what it is you need to overcome. Be clear about your intentions. Be vulnerable with yourself and remember to have fun! You are on a journey! Make your story a memorable one! Don't let fear control you, as in the short story below.

The Unknown

There once was a criminal who had committed a crime, as criminals do. The criminal, sad and dejected at his impending doom, was presented to the king for his punishment. The king told him he had a choice of two punishments; He could either be hung by a rope or take what's behind the big, dark, scary, mysterious iron door. The criminal, terrified of what was lurking behind the cold dark door, quickly decided on the rope. As the noose was being slipped around his neck, he turned to the king and asked: "By the way, sire, as I'm about to die, out of curiosity, what's behind the big dark iron door?" The king laughed and said: "You know, it's funny! I offer everyone the same choice, and nearly all choose the rope." "So," said the criminal, "Tell me. What's behind the door? I mean, I won't tell anyone," pointing to the noose around his neck. The king paused for a moment. "Freedom, my boy, freedom! It seems most people are so afraid of the unknown that they immediately take the rope." And the criminal dropped to his death, taking an unerringly long time to die. Alan Watts said it well when he said: "Our lives are one long effort to resist the unknown."

Butterfly

One day, a small gap appeared in a cocoon, through which a butterfly would appear. A boy who accidentally passed by stopped to watch how the butterfly was struggling to get out of the cocoon. It took a lot of time; the butterfly was trying very hard, the gap not appearing wide enough for the butterfly to free itself. The boy instinctively wanting to save the butterfly took a penknife and cut open the cocoon. The butterfly immediately wriggled out and was free, but its body was weak, her wings barely moving. The boy continued to watch the butterfly, thinking that its wings would spread and she would fly. However, that did not happen. For the

The New Selfish

rest of its life, the butterfly had to drag its feeble body and wings that weren't spread. She would never fly. The boy, because of his ignorance did not know the Butterfly needed to struggle through the narrow gap of the cocoon to free itself, so that the life-giving fluid would move from the body to her wings, enabling her to fly as nature intended. In its wisdom, nature forces the butterfly to leave its shell through the struggle of change, so that it would become stronger in order to grow and develop.

Not unlike the ignorant boy who didn't understand the power of struggle, if we continually avoid inevitable difficulties with indecision and self-doubt, we will not develop our strengths and live to our potential. While venturing into the unknown can be scary, it's not as scary as staying in the same pattern and never truly discovering your worth. We will never learn to "fly", to truly live without coming up against ourselves. No one can do it for us. We can elicit help, but inevitably we must decide to walk our own path and enter the unknown doorways of new experience. If we stay in the known, our lives may be comparatively safe, but are often uninteresting. Adventure means venturing into unknown territories. Think of the most interesting people you may know, or people you've heard stories about. They are most likely courageous and transformative in their nature. They have overcome many obstacles along their path to success. It is not supposed to be easy! If we are to experience ourselves fully, we must take the road less travelled and journey through the dark mysterious doorways of life. We must enter the through the big, dark, scary, mysterious iron door of our weak imaginations to experience freedom on the other side. We must do it with commitment and purpose. If there is something compelling in our life, a purpose, a reason for being, we will take actions to transform the old self. With purpose and passion, almost anything is possible.

Showing Up

The only way that we ever truly learn anything at a core level is through our own personal experiences. Imagine if one of your friends learned to fly. They read all the books, watched videos, practiced on a flight simulator, but never actually got inside of an actual plane. Then one day, after many hours of flight simulation, book reading, and watching videos, they asked if you would like to join them on their first flight? What would you say? I know what I would say! What any normal person would say? Unless you were high on drugs or alcohol, or had a death wish, the answer would be NO! We respect people that have done the thing that we ourselves would like to do. We respect intelligent, courageous people who show up consistently, who make commitments and follow through. In order to truly know yourself, you must commit to your journey. The inner journey of feeling feelings, expressing emotions and being open to what comes through you, and the outer journey to test yourself so you may discover and hone your innate abilities. Testing yourself through experiences in the outer world also creates awareness as to your limitations, where you discover that self-discovery can only be realized from experience. In order to have an experience that you desire, you must therefore make a commitment towards that end. You won't achieve much of anything-just thinking about it. As Joe Dispenza says, "In order to change our personal reality, we have to change our personality". We have to change our attitude towards life. By making meaningful decisions and commitments, we become the alchemist. We change who we are by adopting new attitudes and becoming clear on what we want and WHY! And then we show up and do the work.

Overcoming Adversity

It's amazing what human beings are capable of when we have no choice and have to show up. We have all heard stories of superhuman strength, for example, of a woman lifting a vehicle off of her son, which fell on top of him, as is the story of Angela Cavello in 1982, or in May 1962, Jack Kirby claims a woman lifted a car off her baby, which inspired him to create the "Hulk". In 2006, in Ivujivk, Quebec resident Lydia Angiyou saved several children by fighting a polar bear until a local hunter shot the bear. In 2006, in Tucson, Arizona, Tom Boyle watched as a Chevy Camaro hit 18-year-old Kyle Holtrust. The car pinned Holtrust, still alive, underneath. Boyle lifted the Camaro off the teenager while the driver of the car pulled the teen to safety. In 2009, in Ottawa, Kansas, 5 ft. 7 inch, 185 pound, Nick Harris lifted a Mercury sedan to help a 6-year-old girl pinned beneath. In 2009, in Newport, Wales, Donna McNamee, Abigail Sicolo, and Anthony McNamee lifted a one ton Renault Clio off an 8-year-old boy to save his life. We all have superhuman strengths to overcome the adversities that life can throw our way when there is a big enough WHY! When the desire is stronger than the fear. This is what it means when we say, "we shall overcome". When we commit to something meaningful, we can achieve amazing feats beyond what we ever could have believed possible.

Happiness

As the Dalai Lama points out in his book "The Art of Happiness", happiness is a discipline. It is the quality of your decisions and commitments that will determine the quality of your life. In order for us to experience a genuine sense of self, we must make intelligent commitments. Nothing happens of any actual worth without making commitments, and following through on those commitments. I avoided making major commitments for many years, seeking less challenging paths to make my living, not realizing that my freedom would come from making intelligent commitments that would teach me to overcome fearful thinking. I hope you can learn this lesson sooner than I did! The mindset I adopted out of my ignorance kept me stuck in the same pattern for years. This attitude created a constant state of confusion, indecision, anxiety, and dissatisfaction. I was unaware that I was not valuing myself to show up and do the work and uncover my innate gifts. Because of my indecision and lack of self-worth, I spent years being unhappy and unfulfilled. Because of these denials, I projected this feeling of inadequacy on every relationship I entered, inevitably ending up alone. I unknowingly was living my life with resistance and rigidity based on fears of abandonment from my past. A healthy relationship, whether with your body or with your partner, must have flexibility. BEING OPEN, not closed. I was closed down and did not know it. My first wife was so infuriated; she would physically shake me, imploring me to wake up! Screaming out of desperation for the man she loved. I didn't value myself enough to commit to the processes that would set me free and so I stayed asleep. I hope these words can inspire you to do things differently. Taking an honest assessment of yourself and your results in your life is not an effortless task, and so we avoid true intimacy.

Intimacy

The opposite of commitment is avoidance, which is clothed in fear of intimacy. INTIMACY translates: IN – TO – ME – SEE. Intimacy means being vulnerable and open to examination. Deep inside of ourselves, we are fragile and afraid, and so we hide in our own world, or indulge in behaviors and addictions to avoid feelings we are terrified to feel. It's a horrible way to live! Avoidance, procrastination, laziness, and lack of self-discipline are all based on low self-worth and not valuing your self. By making meaningful commitments, we can overcome the stagnant self and reinvent ourselves to a new way of being. It's sad that so many of us have become detached from our true identity and wallow in a lost world because we don't value ourselves. We are in a human "race" and do not know where we are running, disappearing into avoidance behaviors, addicted to materialism, food, TV, social media, drugs, alcohol, or blaming and condemning others. We will do almost anything to avoid coming up against our self and facing our fears. As in the story of the criminal afraid to enter the cold mysterious dark iron door, we unknowingly "take the rope" and die a slow death.

Overcoming Yourself

If we are to grow beyond the old self and live a purposeful life, then we must courageously transform old ways of unconsciously living and take personal responsibility for the results that show up in our lives. Knowing ourselves more intimately by becoming self aware of our attitudes and behaviors is essential for our growth and well being. If we truly valued ourselves, we would make self-awareness a priority. We can only share that what we are. We can only receive in equal measure to what we can give. How unfortunate that so many live a lost life and never experience their truest self. As Robin Williams quoted in the 1989 movie Dead Poets Society, "Most men lead lives of quiet desperation". By developing your innate gifts and sharing confidently with others (by being present), you are a part of the solution, aligning with your true nature.

Why Low Esteem Affects Meaningful Commitments

If you suffer with a sense of not being enough, and feel stuck, fearful of making a wrong decision, there can be a tendency to impulsively rush into a decision without thinking things through. Tony Robbins says people are happiest when they are progressing. When we feel we are moving forward in our lives, we are happier. This makes sense if you understand that life is movement. When we feel stagnant, and life is not stimulating, we often make a poor decision to feel something, so we can at least pretend we are moving forward. If you are stuck in avoidance behaviors, you can easily make potentially life-changing decisions that may have a negative outcome for the rest of your life. If you don't value yourself and commit to the steps necessary to make intelligent decisions and commitments, you will inevitably suffer the consequences. Short-term fixes can equal long-term misery. Suffering with self-esteem issues, I have sought short-term gratifications in many areas of my life, so I could feel good about myself, because

I didn't. It doesn't work! I can share these insights because of seeking quick fixes, which resulted in pain and suffering, both financial and emotional. My beloved dad said I would learn the hard way, and he was absolutely right! Even if we get lucky, for example in finances, and make quick money, we would not build our character to handle life at a higher level, which is why people who win the lottery, or inherit a fortune, often end up broke. If we truly cared about ourselves, we would nurture our decision-making processes and do the work necessary for a greater chance of a positive outcome. By adopting rules into your decision-making, you can save yourself a lot of unnecessary pain and regret. With that said, let's look at how making commitments works, and how we grow through the process.

The Commitment Experience

1. When we make a commitment to something new, and follow through with an action, we have an experience.
2. The experience gives us increased awareness.
3. As we experience the new awareness, we have a FEELING.
4. The feeling creates an emotion that either feels good, bad, or somewhere in between.
5. The more new experiences we have, the more aware we become by paying attention to how we FEEL.
6. When a similar circumstance (energy) shows up in our life, we can reference experiences, adjust our attitudes and behaviors so we may experience an improved feeling.
7. When we feel good, we make better choices.

8. Better choices increase self-confidence, and so our self-esteem improves.
9. Positive energy reacts to the law of attraction, which opens up new opportunities.
10. New opportunities increase our experiences, which leads to abundance and wisdom.

Why?

Simon Sinek is a well-known British - American author and motivational speaker. He is best known for his TED Talk on "WHY". Why we do what we do is the most important question to answer of ourselves before embarking on a new journey. Simon says, your "Why" comes from within you. It is a feeling that compels you to do the work you want to do, even if it requires sacrifice. You may struggle with thoughts of self-doubt. However, regardless of those sacrifices, you still feel driven to pursue what you really want to do because it gives you meaning. If you know anything about success, it comes with a price! By communicating clearly to yourself why you want to make change and visualizing successful outcomes, you are more likely to overcome old patterns and write a new story. You can't go back and make a brand new start, but you can start from where you are, and make a brand new end!

Doing The Work

A man approached a farmer who was standing on his land, which was covered with beautiful fruits and vegetables graced with all kinds of wonderful colors. The man said to the farmer, "You are

The New Selfish

a lucky man! God has granted you with such a beautiful farm". The farmer contemplated the stranger's remark before replying: "Yes, I am fortunate indeed! But you should've seen it when God had it all to himself!" We must partner with God and work with him to develop our gifts. He cannot do it for you, but he can do it through you. Surrendering to a higher power, to the greater intelligence that permeates all things, is essential to experience wholeness. Whether you are writing a book, entering a new relationship, starting a business, committing to a healthier lifestyle, or whatever the life choice is to improve your current situation, you must partner with your higher power and develop trust and faith along your path. However, trust and faith won't do it alone. We must fully bring ourselves consciously with a strong "WHY" so we can overcome our negativity and do the work patiently as we overcome old patterns. If you are one of those people, as I have been, who does not take time to do the exercises written in the book you are reading, it's for two reasons: You either don't value the material, or you don't value yourself to take the time to assimilate what you are reading by doing the recommended exercises. If you don't value the material, stop reading the book. Perhaps you are not ready to do the work, or the book sucks! If you feel the material is worth your time, then meet the material and yourself with respect and do the work. Whatever it is you are deciding in your life, whatever the beliefs you may have, nothing comes to fruition without joining. Remember the farmer who made his land bountiful? "Your farm is your mind". We can't flourish by living vicariously through other people's experiences, as in watching movies, soap operas, or social media. Like working out at a gym, you have to do the work!

....

Making commitments, whether they turn out good or bad, in the long term can only assist in your personal growth. As you recognize the importance of intelligently making commitments and following through on those commitments, you become more aware of yourself and your limitations, removing the veil of uncertainty as you grow from each experience. When we make a commitment and have an experience, we are no longer stuck in indecision as we now know more through the experience, instead of being stuck thinking about it. Taking actions consequently opens us up to more choices, which, of course, is what FREEDOM represents. You are not stuck in a box like you may think you are; you are only stuck in the box *because* you think you are. There are many choices available to all of us who live in a free world, providing we think and act outside of the box. When assessing future commitments, both on the inner journey of your life, and the outer experiences you are desirous of achieving, you may follow the steps below to achieve more successful outcomes. I have included questions in the areas of personal development, health, business, relationships, and spirituality. You can work with whatever areas you feel are of primary importance. Come back to these questions whenever you feel you need more clarity around a specific area in your life.

Action Steps:

Talk to your camera or journal.

1. Write out clearly WHY you want your desired result? If you are practicing "Camera Talk", talk to your camera or journal about why making commitments in this area of your life is important.

2. How will you feel in the future if you make commitments to achieve your desired result? How will you feel in 5 years and 10 years because you followed through on your commitment and made it successful?
3. How will you feel if you don't follow through, knowing the time will pass? Get leverage on yourself, knowing you don't want to live a life of regret.
4. Take time to do this consistently before going to bed and when you wake up in the morning. Where your attention goes, your energy flows! Visualize your outcomes. Yes, you are hypnotizing and reprogramming your old self to see and be your NEW SELF.
5. Analyze potential obstacles that may present themselves, and how to best protect you in overcoming these challenges. Can you accept the worse case scenarios?
6. Before making the commitment, ask yourself; is it worth it? Will the risk be worth the reward? Can I accept the worse case scenario?
7. If the decision is to move forward, write the "WHY" and read it regularly, and practice # 2 each morning to anchor in your feeling of success.

Personal Development

Action Steps

Below are questions you can consider depending on what area of life you are most interested in improving. You can practice "Camera Talk", or journaling to gain more awareness.

1. What am I afraid of finding out about myself?
2. Why do I want to know myself at a more intimate level?
3. How do I want to be remembered?
4. How can I be more courageous in my life?
5. Am I prepared to be vulnerable with my relationships and myself and what does that look like?
6. What mistakes have I made and what did I learn?
7. What's holding me back from living my dreams?
8. What has been my greatest struggle?
9. What's the scariest thing I've ever done and what did I learn?
10. What scares me most about the future?

Health

Without good health, nothing is going to mean much in your life. Health is number one!

Action Steps

1. Journal, or speak to your camera on WHY your health and well being are of primary importance.
2. Decide on an improved diet and exercise routine. Start the process and follow through. Value yourself to adopt better habits. You are worth it!

3. Listen to role models who encourage you to stay strong through your commitment to better health. When working out, or during other exercise routines, listen to podcasts, YouTube videos, or whatever other media channels that can inspire you to stay on track.

4. Be gentle with you. Don't beat yourself up if you fall off the wagon. Get back on and carry on.

5. Love yourself through the process of change.

Business

Action Steps

1. Come up with three or more choices for your future business goals. Give yourself permission to be creative. You don't have to pigeonhole yourself.

2. WHY? Get clear on WHY this is important to you. If you are desirous of landing a great job, get clear on WHY? If you want to be an entrepreneur, get clear on why? Tony Robbins says business is a spiritual game. The WHY has to mean more than money? Why this business, or this job? What does it mean to you financially, personally, spiritually?

3. Be the pessimist - businesses fail predominately because of insufficient funds, lack of experience in the business endeavor, and lack of leadership skills and poor planning. Get clear on the price you will pay to live your dream. If not, your dream can become your nightmare! Assess potential problems. Do your research! Get REAL. Why and how did other people fail in your particular realm of business? What are the worst case scenarios? Come up with answers to overcome unforeseen challenges. How can you protect yourself against worse case scenarios? Can you accept the worse case situation?

4. Find role models. What are successful people doing in your industry? Read about these people, or study them on YouTube. Seek mentors. Join a mastermind group or start one yourself. Choose carefully. We become the company we keep!

5. Decide on your number one choice. Write the steps to begin your number one choice.
6. Take action immediately, NOW! Make the phone call, or sign up for the class. Do something NOW!
7. Once committed to the process, don't quit, follow through. You will learn something!

Spirituality

I grew up in a household where there was no spiritual practice. The first time I went to church was as a 13-year-old to the local dance. The first time I experienced spirituality was to check out girls in an old English church. Now, I pray, I talk to GOD regularly. I see God in nature and in everything that surrounds me. I believe our relationship with God is personal. In order for me to go deeper into my spirituality, I have embarked upon Ayahuasca journeys, meditation retreats, Church retreats, and other practices to experience a deeper connection. With no spiritual connection, all the other commitments will end up being meaningless. God is trust. When you make a commitment to God, you are making a commitment to trust in the process of life as it unfolds. "The path to awakening is anchored in surrender, not in control!"

Action Steps

1. Write or talk with your camera about what you believe about GOD. Who is GOD, the Universe or whatever noun you would like to use for your higher power? Get clear on your spiritual relationship.

2. What is missing in your spirituality? Is there emptiness within you? When do you feel more connected? What activities bring you closer to GOD and your true self?

3. What activities would you like to practice? Are you meditating? Do you pray? Do you go to Church or other congregations to experience community?

4. What are three areas you can practice connection to your spirituality?

5. What creative activities help you feel more at one, more whole? Choose one and commit to the process.

Relationships

Journaling and "Camera Talk" are especially helpful when dealing with emotional decisions. It is so important to see things, as they are, not how you wish them to be. A healthy relationship can significantly improve your happiness. This is one of the most important choices you will ever make. Entering a partnership or marriage is easy to get into, and not so easy to get out of. Emotional decisions are tricky. Take time and ask a lot of questions of yourself and the relationship. I have been married three times. I've made many mistakes in relationships. What I've learned is a relationship cannot make you whole. You can only bring to the relationship that what you are. If you are a lost soul looking for a solution, then finding a life partner may not be the answer. You soon discover that you are still the unhappy, unfulfilled person who now projects your unhappiness onto the other person, and vice versa with your partner. People love to play the blame game. Drama is a wonderful way to avoid intimacy. If you think someone else is going to make you happy, then you are wrong. The "New Selfish" says you do what you do for you, because of how you feel, not to satisfy another's dysfunction. Work on yourself, not on why the other person needs to work on him or herself. It's always easier to see the other person's issues. Love them, work on you. When you change yourself, the world around you changes. As Michael Jackson said in his song, Man in the Mirror, "I'm starting with the man in the mirror. I'm asking him to change his ways". Look at yourself and make the change.

Action Steps:

Talk to your camera or journal.

1. WHY? Why does this person feel like the right fit? Passion can fade after a time. See yourself in the future. Is this going to be worth the risk? Be honest. Be practical. Do you make a good team? Can you work together? Do you compliment each other? Why is this person the one for you?

2. Be the pessimist so you can avoid negative outcomes before they show their ugly face. Are there patterns in the relationship that need to be looked at now? Don't think they will miraculously go away on their own.

3. Can you deal with worst-case scenarios? How can you protect yourself from worse case scenarios? Can you overcome the challenges? If so, how? Do you need counseling?

4. What's the rush? Do you both need more time? Pressuring a potential partner does not work. When you give space, love shows up. Do you need to make agreements? Is there

The New Selfish

anything not on the table? Are you or your partner hiding something? If you don't deal with it now, it will become much bigger later.

5. Be the Optimist - Look at the best-case scenario. Visualize yourself in the future. How does it feel to overcome the many challenges that life presents, knowing you chose the right partner? How does it feel to know your partner has your back? If children are in your plans, or pets, see yourself into the future.

6. If you are entering a new relationship, and before emotions hypnotize you, ask for a background check. Offer your background check as well. I know this may sound ridiculous to some of you. However, we do background checks when renting a property, buying a car, or applying for a mortgage. Surely, your future happiness warrants the same due diligence. There are a lot of actors out there. Be smart and value yourself!!!

Making intelligent commitments takes time. When you have the luxury of time, make sure you take that time to analyze your decisions before jumping in. Look at all the potential scenarios, both good and bad, and see how and where you can decrease risk. Try not to put your eggs in one basket. Be disciplined when you are making commitments. And conversely, remember that you don't want to over analyze. When you over analyze, you become paralyzed, and may lose the opportunity. If you follow the above guidelines, you can avoid lots of pain. When you make powerful meaningful commitments, you change your life for the better. Once you have done due diligence and make the commitment, then pour yourself into the commitment. We cannot grow beyond

The New Selfish

ourselves without taking risks. Entering the unknown is both scary and exciting. In the next chapter, you will learn the art of "Camera Talk" and why it is helpful to learn methods that can help you become closer and more intimate with yourself. The inward journey is one we must take if we want to live authentically.

Decisions

To decide, to decide, such an aggravation!
I can't decide what train to get on
Let alone what station!
The choices, the choices

All I hear are a thousand voices…
Buy this, buy that, see this one, see that one
Go here, go there…
And then I sigh and take a look…
I find myself going nowhere!

So make your choices and make them clear
Hear your voice, the one beneath the fear
Follow your heart and your dreams will come true
Make your decisions to be all that is you!

CHAPTER 7

"The passage of the mythological hero may be over ground, incidentally; fundamentally it is inward - into depths where obscure resistances are overcome, and long lost, forgotten powers are revivified. The perilous journey is a labor not of attainment but retainment, not discovery but rediscovery."

Joseph Campbell

The Inward Journey Part 1

The practice of going inward quiets our busy mind and connects us to our true nature by surrendering to the present moment. By opening ourselves to the space between our thoughts, we can receive what wants to express itself through us. As Joseph Campbell states, the journey is not of attainment, but retainment, not one of discovery, but one of rediscovery. As we practice surrendering to the now, we connect to our authentic self and discover that learning is remembering. When we remember who we are, we become one with the omnipotent, omniscient, omnipresent source energy that knows. This is when courage is elevated to faith. Integrating your past without judgment and resistance enables you to use your story as a teaching tool for others. No longer addicted to fearful thinking, what we develop on the inside is expressed in the outer world as we join with a higher power that knows no limits. Over time and with practice, we naturally develop the ability to know when and when not to react, to speak, to listen, to take action, to be present without an agenda. By knowing yourself at a deeper level through your inward journey, and the outer expressions to experience your personal growth over time and with practice, you become wise. Because of your nature to be a giver, you are free to live a life without regret. Understanding your history has enabled you to understand both yourself and others, that your story was necessary to awaken you to live your life on purpose.

Pathways To Inner Peace

There are many methodologies available in order to experience more self-awareness on your journey inward, such as Meditation, Journaling, Camera Talk, Yoga, Tai Chi, Chi Gong, Breath Work, Psychedelic medicines, and other practices to increase self-awareness. Several years ago, while practicing Chi Gong, the instructor addressed the class as "Little Dragons". The average age of the participants was 75 years old! And yet he still referred to everyone in the class as a "Little Dragon". He voiced encouragement in his broken English; "Come on, Little Dragons, you can do it!" It was all I could do to not fall on the floor laughing, listening to the little Buddhist monk encouraging

The New Selfish

the "Little Dragons" to bring it on home. Watching older folks moving ever so slowly as they learned Chi Gong was refreshing. The point he was making, of course, is we are all children finding our way back to wholeness. You must be patient with yourself as you embark on your journey. It's not a simple path, and it is not supposed to be. As you know from your own life, your most profound learning has come from difficult times. Pain is a necessary teacher because it forces us to contemplate. It is important to be disciplined with your decisions and commitments. It is also equally important to be gentle with yourself as you navigate your path to wholeness. You must become the observer of your patterns; experiment with new attitudes to see how you feel the next time a similar circumstance arises, remembering that your energy is driving your life. By paying attention to your energy and ensuing reactions, you can consciously grow beyond previous patterns that have been keeping you stuck and unhappy. As your inner world changes, the outer world and your experiences change to match and mirror that you are becoming. The navigation system to change old patterns within is through feelings. By going inward and asking yourself how you felt with each experience, you can adjust your behaviors to evolve beyond the old self. As we embrace this labor of self-love, the easier change becomes. After a while, it won't be a chore anymore. It's a skill that takes time to perfect through coaching, practice and self-monitoring. We must first recognize our patterns and the resistance to change.

Resistance

Resistance shows up when confronted with change, because we are creatures of habit. Change is threatening to the status quo and who we think we are, and who think we are supposed to be.

Deep inside, you know there is something beckoning you to a greater calling. If you don't listen and take intelligent chances of yourself, you will live a life of quiet desperation, allowing fear and doubt to rule your life. Initially, it takes effort and courage to change your predictable life. However, as Ralph Waldo Emerson said, "The whole course of things goes to teach us faith, we need only obey. There is guidance for each of us, and by lowly listening we shall hear the right word". Therefore, initially on your inward journey, you must have patience and a nurturing attitude towards yourself. It takes time, discipline, and practice to overcome old thought patterns. To live a full life, you must leave your comfort zone to grow beyond old behavior patterns. Life is movement, both inner and outer explorations that we must embrace if we wish to be congruent with ourselves. As Tim Robbins character Andy Dufresne said in the movie, "The Shaw shank Redemption", "Get busy living or get busy dying". Movement is life. Inner movement gives life. The inward journey is where change begins.

The Hero's Journey

When going within, especially with meditation, Camera Talk, and psychedelic medicines, you may experience powerful emotions, both painful and joyful. In fact, your feelings are key to knowing WHO YOU are. It's necessary for the energy to work through you to facilitate healing. Purging suppressed energy is transformative and difficult. It is important to embrace the experience and open yourself to surrendering, inviting that what wants to come through. In mythology, we know the inward journey as the "Hero's Journey". The hero leaves the safety of his "home" (the known) and embarks on a journey of self-discovery. When he returns, after being in exile, having overcome many challenges along his path, he returns to a new way of being. By purging blocked energy through many trials, the hero opens to a new way. The hero becomes the hero by overcoming the many challenges on his journey. He doesn't blame others, or hide from his path, but grows from the journey. Your life is an adventure. It is not what you get, but who you become. As this transformation takes place, the more self-acceptance you experience and naturally pass this awareness to others, living your life by example.

We Are Our Own Worst Enemy

The Planet we live on is both beautiful and brutal. Humanity is the same. There is evidence all around us of incredible accomplishments. All you have to do is look around and see what we can achieve. The opposite is also true. The devastation of negative emotions often inherited from our past shows itself in insane ways. Human beings acting out of past transgressions, long buried, do the most awful of deeds to one another. *We are the Gods of unlimited potential and the Devil in our own demise.* What you do to another, you are doing to yourself. It is time to become aware, to awaken to the hero within and overcome the old selfish, ignorant mindset and transcend to a higher state of being. We learn that our true happiness comes from developing our gifts and sharing with others. To the degree that we forget who we were by being present enables each one of us to heal the wounds from the past. When we open ourselves to give without attachments, we naturally open to receive because giving and receiving emanate from the same energy source. Much like that of a river being un-damned, the life force flows freely as we remove the blocks from its natural path. The question becomes; are you ready to be your own hero? Are you willing to experience feelings that will free you from your imprisoned self? The ideas I share in this chapter to experience feelings intimately with yourself through "Camera Talk" and other methods will help release old patterns that are no longer serving you. I also share my experience with meditation retreats and Ayahuasca journeys in Chapter 8 "The Inward Journey, Part 2" which have assisted in my healing both psychologically and physically. In the beginning, this is a private journey that you will undertake to discover who you really are. It's a beautiful experience that can be painful. Letting go of suppressed feelings from the past is necessary so you can live your life now, and not some imprint from the past. When you were born, you were initiated into the hero's journey. It is now time to pick up your sword and awaken to your purpose, to grow beyond the old self. You must have your story; it cannot no longer have you.

Healing

I've learned more about myself during painful times in my life than I ever have from the good times. Whether the experiences were from a relationship, financial decisions that did not go well, or injuries and illness, I learned more through the challenging times than I ever did when life was predictable. When the going gets tough, we ponder upon ourselves. When the upset and anger eventually subsides is when the life lesson becomes apparent. We discover whom we are and what lies deep within when forced to face feelings that can no longer be denied. Pain in the present can often be the karmic effect of pain from the past. When the dust settles, and we contemplate our lives, we can see how much we grew from the experience. Eckhart Tolle says that the world was not created to make us happy, it is supposed to make us grow! When presented with a challenging situation, we learn and grow from adversity. Like it or not, this is our evolution. We are best to accept our own personal life story and be conscientious writers of our story. All grand stories have adversity embedded within them where the protagonist, in some manner or another, overcomes difficulty. In doing so, we become the hero of our own story. As a friend recently pointed out to me, every master was once a disaster! What have you learned from your painful experiences? What would you do differently knowing what you now know? How could you help others avoid the pitfalls that you have experienced? The self-help industry is growing exponentially with people just like you and me that have knowledge that can save another pain. According to recent statistics, as of the writing of this book, the self-help business has revenues of 13.2 billion dollars per annum in the USA, and growing. Because of social media, the average person can use their personal learning experiences to create educational courses as teaching tools for others. It's a massive growth business with huge potential. As you help others, your story becomes the transformative healing energy for yourself as well. Perhaps there is a business endeavor whereby you can reap the rewards of your life lessons and help others avoid costly mistakes in whatever area of expertise you have struggled in? This is one way to transform your story into something worthwhile and live a purposeful life.

Time To Wake Up

During my early thirties, while dating a young woman whom I was very much in love with, she unexpectedly broke up with me.

She turned from being a loving, kind, and funny girl to cold and uncaring. She was done with me, and it hurt. I didn't know where to turn or what to do? I realized I needed to spend quality time to understand what had happened? I became aware (using my camera) that I had buried deep feelings that were not about my girlfriend. I realized the feelings of grief and abandonment were not about her, but about my mum leaving home many years prior when I was a boy. This recognition was a revelation, as I realized my girlfriend leaving me was actually a gift. I was no longer a victim of circumstance, but the receiver of new awareness that could free me from past pain. I explained this revelation to myself as I spoke to my camera. I realized my girlfriend was the catalyst necessary to awaken me from a buried past that was emotionally driving my life. Dr. Joe Dispenza says; "You can't change your mind at the same level of awareness the problem was created from". We must process the experience though a different filter, and become the observer from a different vantage point, so we may awaken from the conditioned past. Upon this realization, I felt a deep love for my girlfriend and was no longer angry, even though I was reeling from the abandonment, knowing that what she did in breaking up was exactly what I needed. This recognition created both deep sadness for the loss, and joy for the knowing. I had buried the pain from my mother leaving home deeply within since I was a little boy. This angry, toxic energy had dictated all of my relationships. I was angry with women and never knew it? What felt like a devastating loss turned out to be the perfect opportunity to begin my inward journey, which was when I began "Camera Talk". During my sessions, I cried, laughed, and philosophized. I talked to my camera for six months, almost every night. I realized meeting other women, or whatever other distractions, would not solve my issues. I began the process with my camera, realizing that I was the problem, and no other person could heal me but me. I knew it was time to go within and let go of what was no longer working in my life. I would sit with my dog and watch the recordings of David speaking to David, where I would cry, laugh and sometimes get up and dance as I observed the young man speaking back to me, who was me! I started "Camera Talk" over 30 years ago. You will discover, as I did, that you never tire of knowing yourself more deeply.

Camera Talk

If you are like most people, you have a constant chatter going on in your head, of which mostly you are unaware. The human heart beats 100,000 times per day, pumping as much as 2000 gallons of blood through our system without conscious awareness. Our thinking 95% of the time is also unconscious. The thoughts coming from your unconscious are the driving force and navigation system for your life's path. It would seem beneficial then to actually know what you are saying to yourself, so that you consciously direct your life in the direction that you want to go, instead of following the navigation system of some past belief system that you mostly inherited. Human evolution is the application of awareness within our environment and within our self. All technological advances had the intrinsic laws in place prior to their discovery. However, the awareness was not accessible prior to those discoveries. The laws of the universe have always been the same. The awareness of those laws was not at our disposal until we discovered them. This is the same truth within you! The question becomes then, how can you attain more awareness, and consequently make use of the

The New Selfish

laws of the universe that are already in place and waiting for you to tap into? Your greatness, your beauty, your uniqueness, your authenticity, your brilliance, your magnificence; it has always been there lying dormant within. You are a part of the wholeness of the one intelligence that permeates all of life. You are that one! The secret to your freedom lies within you, to know you. And when you do, the limitations fall away. You are the diamond deep beneath the earth's crust that requires your own mining. It is beliefs from experiences, and inherited beliefs from your ancestry that make you believe something completely different. The voice that says, "I'm not good enough", or whatever the self talk is that negates our true value ". The truth inside of you knows this is not true! You are a unique manifestation of the divine that wants to express through you. Your cup runs over when you get the small you out of the way and allow what wants to come through you without judgment or attachment. Recognition comes more easily as you practice being in the moment, allowing the divine energy within to transform the old you. This is what it means to be reborn. This is the beginning of a new path, one that opens up by knowing yourself intimately. What I am suggesting is that you can begin the journey by talking to a camera. It's easily accessible, you can do it in your home, in your car (not while driving) or in any place you can have privacy.

Why Camera Talk Works

In psychology, they call this type of therapy "Free Association". Free association, originally developed by Sigmund Freud, expresses consciousness without censorship as an aid in gaining access to unconscious processes. "Camera Talk" is a perfect method to become conscious of what lies within. To truly know you is to love yourself, which is the ultimate experience of self-acceptance. "Camera Talk" is an intimate way to connect to you through the lens of a camera. There are, of course, other methods to have a more intimate journey of this life through such means as talking to a mirror, journaling, writing poetry, meditation, and other creative methods to discover more of whom you are. The reason I advocate talking to a camera is it works and is easy to do. You can also play back your recordings to see your growth. Michael Singer, author of the "Untethered Soul" and the "Surrender Experiment" discusses how there are two of us inside of our heads. There is the one doing the talking and there is the one doing the listening or observing. Most of us don't talk to ourselves in a way that encourages us to be the best version of our self. Unfortunately, the voice inside of us is often berating or judging. Our self-talk feeds our energy system, which affects our well being and quality of life. It is not what you eat that makes you who you are; it is primarily your beliefs and your thinking that determine your experience. Your thinking is a honing device that dictates your future. With this knowledge, it's very important that we protect our thinking against negativity, which is incessant and often inherited from the past. If you truly want to live a new life, you must break the chains from toxic thinking. Talking to yourself through the lens of the camera enables you to connect to yourself consciously by bridging the gap between you and your thoughts.

The Gap

There's a great deal of discussion today in the scientific and metaphysical communities about "space". The cells in our bodies comprise mostly of space. We live in a universe made up mostly of space, and our planet is rotating in the middle of space. The gap between our thoughts is also space. We are told we think between 60,000 to 80,000 thoughts a day that traverses space before becoming a thing. We are constantly reminded that thoughts are things. Everything you see around you in the physical world began with a thought. In meditation, we sit in stillness and let thoughts drift pass as if clouds passing through space, practicing non-attachment to our thoughts and encouraged to focus on the emptiness, on the space. When practicing "Camera Talk" you are putting space between you and your thoughts. Wayne Dyer referred to space as the gap between our thoughts. He said that we need the void of nothing-in order to create something. As an example, consider any sound that you might make. Where does it come from? It comes from the void, the silence. Without the gap, without the void, there would only be noise. The precious present moment is the gap between the noise. Joe Dispenza says we are continuously keeping our life the same because we are keeping our attention (thoughts) and our energy (feelings) the same. In his meditation retreats, Joe encourages his students to enter into the black space of the unknown. During his meditations, Joe constantly talks of "space", where all change takes place. Just as sound comes from the void, our creations are born from the unknown, from the emptiness, from the space. When talking to a camera, you are putting space between your thoughts and what comes back to you. You are on the other side of the camera as the receiver of your thoughts and your messages back to you. When we are in our unconscious thinking (thoughts) we berate and judge ourselves (feelings). When we talk to a camera, because there is more conscious awareness and space between our thoughts,

The New Selfish

we can consciously talk to ourselves gently, with honesty, as if talking to a close friend. We are more aware of how we are feeling when talking to our self. When observing your recordings, you can be present with yourself and listen as you share what's most important. You are becoming conscious of yourself, your thoughts, and how you feel.

How Camera Talk Works

In most of my "Camera Talk" sessions, I would often start seriously, talking about the issues in my life; business, relationships, and why I was feeling disconnected. After a while, I became bored with the same dour, dark energy that was regurgitating itself through my consciousness. After wallowing in my unhappiness, I would become bored, and so I would get up and dance, or become a character to entertain myself; a Jew, a Chinaman, a German, a Gay guy, or whatever I felt like doing to feel free and laugh. After all, no one was going to view the recordings but me. This is not something I am going to post on Facebook. These intimate recordings were for my eyes only. I was free to be myself without the filters and negative self-talk. It's incredibly freeing to be silly and have fun not worrying about what someone may or may not think, as well as talking seriously about the important matters of life. Talking to my camera has helped me to express myself freely and connect authentically without beating myself up about the past and what I cannot change. When I play back the recordings, I feel connected, listening to what my inner self knows to be true. For me, it relaxes me, providing a sense of peace as I listen to the truth that I already know, but never listen to. Talking to your camera may sound narcissistic, but it really is not. Being authentic is not narcissistic; it's necessary for your happiness and health. "Camera Talk" is an excellent method of practicing being at one with yourself, and letting go through self-expression.

The Groove

While practicing "Camera Talk" you may experience, as I have done, the feeling of being in the "groove". The "groove" is when you are so connected that time stands still; there is no sense of self-consciousness. When you are in the groove, your consciousness flows through the lens of the camera directly back to you. When you watch the recording, you feel aligned with yourself and with what you are sharing. You will have an experience of feeling at one, both during the recording and while playing the recording back. The truth is the truth. It sets you free! The benefit of this practice is that you can share from your authentic self, instead of being ego driven. It is important to understand that this is a practice like any other. The more you practice, the more you will feel at one with who you are. Just as the example of a top-notch entertainer who is comfortable in their own skin sharing their gift, so it will be with you. Your authentic self will naturally come to the forefront in your life as you practice becoming more at one with who you really are. You are that never ending spring of life that constantly wants to give of yourself. You cannot give from an empty cup. You must fill your cup up first, and then all good will come from that space. As Shakespeare's character Polonius quoted in Hamlet: "To thine own self be true, and it must follow as the night the day, thou canst not then be false to any man."

How to Begin

I began "Camera Talk" over 30 years ago, which was a more arduous process than it is today. With smart phones, everything is so simple. If you don't have privacy in your home, you can always go for a drive, park your vehicle, and have a conversation with your camera. No one questions this because we are talking on our phones all the time. If possible, I would suggest you find a comfortable space in your home where you have privacy. When speaking to the camera, it is best to focus on the lens of the camera. I have found that when I reverse my camera, so I'm looking at myself while talking to the camera, this can be distracting. My intention is to be in the moment with myself and watch the recording in the same manner. I place a book or piece of paper over my image so as not to see myself while speaking and focus on the lens of the camera. I also use a camera case with a flip stand so I can place the camera on my desk when filming. I don't use special lighting or an additional microphone. Most smart phones are sufficient for this exercise. However you decide to record yourself, the focus should be to talk directly to the lens of the camera, imagining yourself on the other side of the lens. One thing to mention here, for whatever your reasons, you may feel like this exercise is not for you. I would suggest trying it to see how you feel.

Camera Talk Steps

1. Speak honestly to yourself by using your first name. Talk using your name and YOU as the noun. For example: "David, you know YOU are being resistant to change. How

The New Selfish

long are YOU going to keep yourself stuck?" ALWAYS call yourself by your name and refer to yourself using the noun YOU. Remembering you are talking to you by separating yourself from yourself.

2. Decide what subject it is you want to discuss with yourself to have more awareness. It could be your work life, personal life, health, or understanding your purpose for being here and what makes you happy. Whatever the subject is that you are struggling with, or want to gain more insight, focus, surrendering to what wants to come through you.

3. Don't judge or berate yourself for past behaviors or current circumstances. You are talking to your best friend, which from this point forward is you! Give yourself the gift of understanding and forgiveness. Be your own best friend!

4. When talking to yourself, focus on how you feel. Try to get out of your head and into your feelings. If you are passionately talking to yourself, this shows you are entering the "groove". You may feel angry, frustrated, joyful, happy, whatever the feeling is - be honest with yourself. The answers will come to you as you become more present. Below is an example of a "Camera Talk" session about how frustrated I've been in getting a business off the ground.

5. "David, you know you're feeling stuck in this business. You've been working on this project now for several years! You know you're frustrated, and you're taking the frustrations out on your relationship. It's not worth it. Give yourself another year; don't focus on the negatives. If you have to let it go, then move on and know you gave

The New Selfish

it your best shot. You're very courageous to take the kinds of chances that you do. Give yourself credit. Decide what to focus on and make a new plan. Life is too short! Give yourself one more year. If you don't see any progress, then cheap sell everything and move on". You never know, maybe you'll become a best-selling author!"

6. Talk about whatever comes to your mind! When you give thoughts space and awareness, they have less power over you, because they are now being given to the light. In "Camera Talk", you are shining a light on the unknown driving forces of your life. As you gain more awareness, you gain more freedom!

7. Be patient. Connecting with you on an intimate level takes practice. This is a nurturing process of loving yourself through honesty and intimacy.

8. Commit to "Camera Talk" sessions several times per week. You are talking to yourself all the time. Make your conversations conscious? "Camera Talk" sessions can be as short or long as you want. Understand that you are in process, accepting what comes through you without judgment.

9. When you experience an "aha" moment, talk about your new awareness. Remember, you are following your stream of consciousness as you become more aware.

10. When you playback the recording, don't judge you! Listen to yourself, because you know you better than anyone else. Are you being authentic? Are you telling yourself a story? Be honest.

The New Selfish

11. It's OK to pay attention to how you look. However, pay attention as an interested observer, not as someone judging you. For example, when I talk to my camera these days, I observe I am looking older. I can embrace my older years and how I look without judging myself. When you accept and embrace your current self, your outer self radiates the same loving energy.

Talking to your camera is a practice in surrendering and being authentic with yourself. This is when the unconscious becomes conscious, and you become one with your stream of thinking. It is an experience that will free you to be who you are without the negative self-talk. As you build trust by being intimate and honest with yourself, and if you have not done so already, you can take your inner journey to the next level through meditation retreats, or perhaps Ayahuasca journeys, as I have done. I share experiences in the next chapter of going deeper into my own inner world and how processing the past and letting go can feel. If FEAR is your guiding light, I suggest extinguishing that flame, as it is a path to nowhere. Turn your attention instead to faith and trust. You are on a journey with an endpoint, where you will leave this place we call home. Make the best use of your time here, and take intelligent risks of yourself to discover more of whom you are.

The Road less Travelled

It is the road less travelled that I seek
For I know it is not travelled by the meek
With a smile on my face and a tear in my eye
It is the road I will travel till the day that I die

CHAPTER 8

> "Your outer journey may contain a million steps; your inner journey only has one: The step you are taking right now."
>
> *Eckhart Tolle*

The Inward Journey Part 2

There is a fear known as "Neophobia", which means to be fearful of anything new. For most of us, it's easier to stay with the same habits and behaviors than to try something new. According to Tony Robbins, there are six human needs if not satisfied, cause unhappiness. The first of these needs is CERTAINTY. Tony is referring to Maslow's theory of human needs, a roof over your head, food in your belly, and some nooky, if you're lucky! Your number one need for safety and security doesn't want you to step out of your comfort zone and take unnecessary risks. The need for certainty sends a message to your brain that says; "safety is number one, and don't forget it! Stay safe and don't rock the boat". Can you see then why Eckhart

Tolle is saying what he's saying? The fear of the unknown can debilitate a person if we do not proceed with conscious intention-the intention to take one step at a time, and be present with each step, because that is the step that matters now. Overcoming your fears is an important part of going inward and deserves respect. You must come up against yourself by being present with each new experience and nurture yourself through the process. We can't expect to change and improve ourselves by doing the same thing over and over and expecting a different result. Change is inevitable and should be embraced. The good news is the SECOND HUMAN NEED, according to Tony, is "VARIETY", meaning, YOU NEED CHANGE! If you feel uncomfortable doing something you've never done before, good! That's where all the good stuff lies, beneath the surface of your comfort zone. One of the most effective ways to elicit change is psychedelic medicine. These substances are not for everyone and should be considered carefully. However, if you feel you're being called to experience plant medicines, then I would suggest researching the subject to gather more information. I share my own experiences with Ayahuasca below. My personal journeys have been quite difficult, largely because I had suppressed feelings for a long time, feelings that needed to be purged so I could live a new life, not an imprint from the past.

Psychedelic Medicine

Psychedelic medicines such as Psilocybin, Ketamine and Ayahuasca are gaining more acceptance as treatments for depression, post-traumatic stress disorders and other mentally related issues. The Texas legislature recently passed a bill to study psilocybin as a treatment for PTSD. 114,000 suicides are a sad statistic for veterans since 2001 in the USA. Clearly pills and talk therapy are not doing the job. Initial studies of psilocybin for mental health are very encouraging. I have not used Psilocybin or "Magic Mushrooms" as referred to in the 60s. My personal experience with hallucinogenic medicine is Ayahuasca. I have experienced both brutal and beautiful journeys. I wouldn't change any of them. Ayahuasca is a mother energy that may not give you what you think you want, but it will give you what you need. As the Rolling Stones song goes, "You don't always get what you want, but you get what you need!" And like some medicines, you may not like the "taste" of what you need. Is Ayahuasca difficult? Short answer - YES! Is it worth it? YES!!! Deep meditation is great too, as is breath work to release trapped energy. It takes work and commitment to let go. There are people in the Ayahuasca community that make claims that one Ayahuasca journey is the equivalent of 10 years of talk therapy. Mother Ayahuasca gives you what you need. It may not feel good, but the experience and insights are, as the Master Card ads state, priceless! If you want to take a journey into your inner world, then Ayahuasca is definitely a pathway for increased awareness.

Ayahuasca - PTSD

I have met several United States veterans who have suffered from debilitating posttraumatic stress disorders. It's wonderful to hear their stories and how Ayahuasca has helped improve the quality of their lives. One man said he went from wanting to kill everybody to wanting to HUG everybody. Isn't that great! Many of these participants are off their medications! These young brave men seem happy and well adjusted to normal life. There is a documentary on Amazon Prime named "From Shock to Awe" that follows the lives of two such men. However, we didn't have to be in a war to develop PTSD. As children, parents or caregivers traumatized many of us. Traumatic events experienced growing up not treated at the causation level will continue to manifest in our adult life. Ayahuasca can help release these patterns, although it may be difficult. For me, the risk is worth the reward.

My Journeys

My 50th birthday was both challenging and awakening after experiencing a panic attack at the Pannikin restaurant in Encinitas, California, where Dr. Love had treated me. Ten years later, about to have my 60th birthday, I travelled to Costa Rica to partake in an Ayahuasca ceremony. It's not what most people would do on their 60th birthday. However, I felt a need to let go of what was keeping me stuck and so booked the trip. In my experience, Ayahuasca has a tendency to "call you" when you're ready. As I boarded the plane and made myself comfortable for the upcoming journey, I closed my eyes, recalling the first time I had experienced Ayahuasca fifteen years earlier during a winter snowstorm in Boston. My girlfriend at the time and her doctor friend Charlene, were hosting a ceremony along with her friend, an American Shaman. The ceremony was to take place on the top floor of the doctor's home in Boston, which was a 100-year-old 4-story building, located across the street from the Atlantic Ocean.

The weather was bitter cold with gale force winds rocking the old house back and forth as we ascended the stairway to embark on what was to be my first Ayahuasca experience. I was nervous and unsure of what exactly I was getting myself into, but went for it anyway, knowing at some point the journey would end. They had made beds ready for Charlene and me while the Shaman and my girlfriend sat across from the two of us to help monitor our journey. Charlene and I made ourselves warm and comfy beneath our respective bed covers, waiting for the ceremony to begin. Snuggling under the covers can feel so good when the weather howls outside. We're back to childhood, safe, warm and loved.

The Shaman was a burly man with sandy colored hair, dressed in faded jeans and a green sweatshirt, a Santa Claus hat atop his head, more resembling an Irish laborer than a spiritual leader. Feeling uncomfortable, wanting to make conversation, I had asked him why he believed in the spirit world? What was it that had him convinced there was something greater than what we perceived? I was interested in why he believed so deeply in Ayahuasca? "Experience!" he exclaimed! Experience! He explained that after hundreds of journeys, having had many transcendent moments, he had no doubts about its existence. It was not a question of faith, but of his experience through the medicine that made him aware of his own inner being and its deeper connection. I was about to be inducted into what he was referring to.

As the plane travelled down the runway, I drifted back to the cold Bostonian evening, the Shaman giving blessings to the spirits prior to pouring the medicine. Yuck! I could still remember the rancid taste. The wind was whistling outside. I could see snowflakes through the small octagonal windows. I pulled the covers over my head and waited. I was nervous and unsure what I was getting myself involved with? I heard weird snoring noises? I peeked over the covers to see the Shaman snoring, his bobble on his Christmas hat in perfect rhythm with his large red nose

The New Selfish

snorting un-pleasantries. I laughed to myself before disappearing beneath the covers, waiting for the medicine to take its effect. Charlene was across from me in her bed, buried under her own covers. My journey began with visions. I was in a jungle. Charlene was gazing into my eyes. She was not in human form, but a magnificent lioness with a mass of red hair flowing down her back, beauty and strength personified as a glorious animal. I couldn't see her physically, as we were both buried beneath our respective blankets, but I could see her spiritual form. She exuded confidence, beauty, and power as a magnificent lioness the like of which I had never seen. *By now, any women reading this are researching Ayahuasca ceremonies on their phone. And I think you should. We need more powerful women in this world.* Charlene shouted to me from across the room. "Do you see me?" "Yes!" I replied, "I see you!" She yelled back in a strong, confident voice, "Don't be afraid! Enjoy your journey!" And she turned from me, a flash of red hair bounding into the jungle. I travelled with my visions, great love embodying forgiveness for myself, and the others I had held in contempt for so long. I felt deep love and compassion, even for the man who was with my ex-wife! I was good with it all. After 4 hours, the journey came to an end. The following morning, after a long walk along the oceanfront, the crisp sound of snow crunching beneath our feet, the clear blue sky with no limits, Heather, Charlene and I laid on our backs giggling as we made angel figures in the snow. It was a heart felt experience of love and gratitude that I never forgot. Costa Rica, I was going to discover, would not be as forgiving.

Costa Rica

I arrived at San Jose airport where the facilitators, Matthew and Jeanae, were waiting to take me to their retreat. Matthew, the Shaman, was an American who conducted ceremonies together with his wife, Jeanae. They had met at a rehab clinic where they were both treated for drug addictions. Matthew's experience with Ayahuasca led him to live in Peru for five years, where he studied shamanism. He was no longer addicted to drugs and alcohol, of which he had been addicted from the age of fifteen. Matthew is a talented musician, and truly living his calling as a shaman. Both him, and Jeanae were free from addictions. They are wonderful examples of how to transform your story and teach others. Besides myself, there were two other participants who were partaking in the ceremony, a young 23-year-old man from San Francisco, and a Scotsman who was an offshore fisherman. The young man would have beautiful experiences on his journeys, full of love and wonder. This was not so for the Scotsman and me.

The First Ceremony

The ceremonial building was on a 20-acre estate, surrounded by nature, with a view of the city lights in the distance. The environment was peaceful and serene. On the first night, I made myself comfortable in my room, which had a private bathroom, where I would end up spending much of my stay. The following evening was the first of two ceremonies, which took place in the studio on one side of the building. There was an eerie silence as the three of us made ready for the upcoming ritual. Nervousness is palpable, especially for those not yet inducted into the ways of

The New Selfish

the medicine. Prior to drinking the brew, the three of us took part in an integration ceremony where we stepped outside into the night air and bathed in flower water as Matthew gave blessings to the spirits. Once back in the ceremony room, we made our way to our mats and awaited instruction. Matthew called our names one by one to sit across from him and drink the medicine, which was given to us in a shot glass.

I remembered the last time I had drunk from a shot glass while vacationing in Cancun, Mexico, at Carlos' n Charlie's. The tourists, of which I was one, would stand in line, whereupon the bartender would bang each of us on the head with a plastic bottle as we downed the local tequila while singing Mexican songs. From what I can remember, it was great fun until the following morning. Ayahuasca was not Carlos' n Charlie's, although getting banged on the head was a metaphor of things to come. The best way I can describe the taste of the Ayahuasca medicine is that of chocolate shit. There is no sugarcoating the taste. It tastes horrible. After drinking the medicine, we laid down on our mats waiting for the effects to kick in. Matthew also drank the medicine as he sang beautiful songs while playing a variety of instruments. I was grateful for the music and the sound of his magical voice vibrating through the room. My throw up bucket close by, I anxiously awaited the medicine's effects. It was my birthday! 60 years old! Where did it all go? Matt, the young man from San Francisco, interrupted my reverie by throwing up. I was feeling nothing. The Scotsman was next, making a loud regurgitating noise as he struggled to let go. Jeanae approached me, asking if I would like to drink more medicine, as I was not feeling its effects. I had heard stories where the medicine could take an hour or more to kick in, and so I declined, deciding to wait, which turned out to be a wise decision.

And then it hit, a wave rushing over me. I immediately got up from my mat and made my way to my room, sensing I was in for something more than I had bargained for. I was afraid, fractal images dancing in front of me as I walked unsteadily towards my room. There was no turning back now. I was in it. I made it to my room, where I headed straight for the bathroom. I would hug the cold porcelain toilet for the next 4 hours, coming face to face with me, and the weight I had dragged around for many years. It was time to let it all go. I purged, and I purged. In between incessant throwing up, I could hear the Scotsman roaming around the garden outside of my room, like a wild animal in deep pain, talking to himself, regurgitating the past; throwing up all that had come before. We were brothers in our own personal pain. Letting go is never easy. I was continually throwing up through my mouth and nose, having to sit on the toilet with frequent, what seemed like never ending bowel movements. On a rare occasion, I would slowly raise my head to look at the hallucinogenic image in the mirror that was I, wondering what kind of birthday was this? And then I was back at it again. I couldn't wait for it to end. The journey lasted four tortuous hours. I was exhausted and swore I would never do it again.

The Next Day

The next morning at breakfast, I sat across from the Scotsman, who looked pale and beaten. Mother Ayahuasca had her way with him, too. He was an unusual fellow, somewhat scholarly, having read books such as the Iliad and the Odyssey and a variety of

The New Selfish

psychology books and other reads of what you would not associate upon meeting him. I inquired if he was going to do the ceremony the following day? He had suffered badly, as I, and was wondering what his answer would be? I was praying he would say no, so that I wouldn't be the only coward backing out. He assured me he had received all and more of what he had come for and would not take part in the Sunday ceremony. His words were soothing to me. We were both beaten from the tortuous night before, akin to the beaten pugilists, who finally hung up their gloves. I wholeheartedly agreed, nodding my head vigorously with his every word. We planned to explain our reasoning to Matthew, our tails between our legs, hoping he would understand - praying he would understand. With new found confidence, reveling in my upcoming escape from any more suffering of the dreaded chocolate medicine, and in a moment of risk, I heard myself exclaiming to my new Scottish friend why I thought he was gaining all of his intellectual knowledge through his many books. That he was using his intellect as a protection, to avoid feeling his feelings. He sat in contemplation with this newfound knowledge, gazing into me, as if questioning the Englishman's intent. I was unsure if I had offended him? The Scots don't really like the English too much. I had suffered enough and was wishing I had kept my mouth shut.

After what seemed like an eternity, he slapped his hand on the breakfast table and exclaimed in his Scottish brogue, "You're right! You're fucking right! I'm not reading another book!" At which point he changed his mind and decided on the second ceremony! Oh no, I thought. His entire demeanor changed as he began proclaiming his love for an English woman he was involved with back home in his beloved Scotland. He swore an oath right there at the breakfast table that he would not let her go, and would ask for her hand in marriage. He had his revelation and was afraid of nothing now. I sat at the breakfast table, head in hands, dreading more of what I experienced the night before. I knew I couldn't quit-me and my big mouth!

The Second Ceremony

The second ceremony took my life away. I physically experienced death. It was the most helpless feeling I've ever endured. The vomiting was more severe than I could have ever imagined. After 4 hours of purging, I lost feelings to my extremities and could not move. I lied down on my bed and let death take me. The experience of feeling that of a 90-year-old man, slowly, painfully feeling the life force abandon my body was like nothing I'd ever experienced. I cried and cried, weeping over my lost life, asking for God's forgiveness. I didn't want to die. After hours of throwing up and looking at my excrement, I finally laid down to surrender. What a sad, lonely way to go is what I thought as a wiped away the flood of tears. What a terribly failed life I had led. The life force ebbed away as I went deeper into nothing. Unbeknownst to myself, I was dying to the old and being born to the new. After what seemed to be an eternity, I felt the life force course back through my body. After five tortuous hours, I rose from my bed and walked outside, steadying myself with each step; tears of joy flooding my face. I looked upwards where the black night sky and the many stars welcomed me, the green grass beneath my feet, cool and free. I made my way to the fire pit where Matt and the Scotsman were sitting in deep thought. I slumped into an awaiting chair and stared deeply into the flickering flames, so grateful to be alive. I breathed the fresh air and smiled.

There is transformation in suffering, in rituals, and rites of passage. It's never easy. The three of us were at peace that night, joined by the knowing of what we had been through. We were brothers in mother Ayahuasca.

Why Suffer?

Why would someone in his or her right mind go through such an ordeal voluntarily? Isn't life painful enough? And I would answer with a rhetorical question: Are we in our right minds? We live in a world that has conditioned us to believe that insanity is normal, where atrocities are justified by inherited beliefs that, when questioned, have no genuine answers, except to reference books written by other humans also suffering from an inherited past. Releasing suppressed energy is difficult and not to be taken lightly. When we read about near-death experiences, we learn from the people who went through these ordeals that when they come out the other side; they see life differently. The ignorance and greed of the human race, with its righteousness, opposes all that we truly are. We are all in this together. To know yourself, for who you really are, beneath the beliefs that limit your experience, has to be transformed if we are to live harmoniously. Ayahuasca is a ritual, a passage of rite that helps transcend the old. The experience can be difficult, and beautiful, as is life itself. I have since experienced Ayahuasca ceremonies, none of which were anywhere close to my Costa Rica experience. In subsequent journeys, I have experienced fractal images, messages for my life, intense grieving for my family and friends, and the camaraderie only realized with mutual understanding of the Ayahuasca experience. Ayahuasca is not for everybody. It is something to investigate, making sure you are a candidate for the medicine. Certain physical and mental challenges may prohibit your ability to undergo an Ayahuasca journey and should be considered before drinking the medicine.

Meditation

Mindfulness and meditation have become increasingly more popular as we attempt to deal with our busy lives in a mad world. For myself, meditation helps to quiet my mind before beginning my day. On a deeper level, I have experienced weeklong retreats with Dr. Joe Dispenza. Joe is the Tony Robbins of the meditation world. What Tony does on the outside, Joe does on the inside. People from all walks of life go to Dr. Joe's retreats for healing and personal growth. He conducts weeklong retreats all over the world. If you can afford to go, they are definitely worth experiencing. Joe, whose background is that of a chiropractor, researcher, neuroscientist and expert in epigenetics and quantum physics, believes that in order to change your personal reality, you literally have to change your personality? Joe says that for genuine change to occur, we effectively have to become a new person and grow beyond the old self. Psychologists tell us that by the time we're in our mid-30s, our identity is formed. This means that for those of us over 35, we have memorized a select set of behaviors, attitudes, beliefs, emotional reactions, habits, skills and memories, and conditioned responses that are now subconsciously programmed within us. These programs, Joe says, are running our life because the body has become the mind. This means that we think the same thoughts, feel the same feelings, and react the same way. Since the body becomes the unconscious mind, it's easy to see that in situations where the body becomes the mind, the conscious mind no longer has much to do with our behavior. Joe explains we react from past conditioning, based on a set of beliefs we are not consciously aware. It's our job then to deprogram ourselves from limiting beliefs by being consciously aware of our thoughts and behaviors. We can practice allowing ourselves to respond instead of reacting unconsciously. Meditation provides the space within your busy mind to calm your thoughts and be present.

Weeklong Retreats

During weeklong retreats with Dr. Joe, I experienced many insights that were definitely big "aha" moments. Each meditation session can last for up to four hours. At the end of the retreat, on the last day, Joe conducts healing meditations. For the participants who feel a need for healing, either physically or emotionally, groups of eight people surround each person who volunteered for the experience. Many volunteers requesting healing have severe illnesses. I wanted to be one of the eight healers surrounding the subject, as well as experience the effects of healing. What I experienced in both scenarios was powerful. What I realized about myself was that it was easier to give than to receive. Receiving means being vulnerable, whereas when giving, I am in control. Like laughing and crying, giving and receiving are two sides of the same coin. You can only do one as well as you can do the other. The combined energy of hundreds of healers in a room focusing their energy with the same intention is quite phenomenal. When we collectively tap into our source, healing occurs. My experience was that of every sinew in my body shaking, floods of tears streaming down my face as I experienced deep release. As I surrendered to the loving energy allowing the feelings to flow through me, feelings of unconditional love bathed my entire being. During the healing sessions, I experienced deep emotions as the giver and the receiver. During Dr. Joe's retreats, participants claim to experience healings from blindness, cancer, and other severe disabilities that conventional medicine could not heal. Joe says that healing occurs when the patient feels so ecstatic in their meditation experience that they lose all attachment to whether or not they get better. The experience during the meditations is so euphoric that they literally forget who they are? And that is when healing occurs, when they let go of the attachments; they are so present in the moment that there is no future or past, when all expectations, all attachments, all judgments, all resistance, all fears and weak imaginations; when all of it is gone but the precious present moment-that's when the miracles occur, when we allow the truth to free us.

My first weeklong retreat with Joe was in Cancun, Mexico. After the healing sessions on the last day, I felt free from anxiety, which I had suffered with for most of my adult life. The following day, I flew back to Tampa, via Atlanta, where I entered through the security line prior to boarding the plane. I'm used to being checked by the airport security as I have a metal hip, and so the alarm activates when I walk through the detection machine. My normal protocol is to point to my hip, where the security officer checks me out with his detection device. I then proceed through the security gate to collect my bags. Something very different occurred. As normal, I walked through the metal detector where the beeping sound activated. I pointed to my hip, explaining to

The New Selfish

the officer of my prosthesis, except this time the security officer said, "I'm not looking at your hip, sir. I'm looking at your head!" Confused, I said, "I'm sorry, I don't understand?" He turned me around and had me look at the image on the machine. The image of my head was bright white, glowing like a light bulb? He waved the detector around my head, found nothing, shrugged his shoulders and waved me through. I asked; "Have you ever seen anything like that before?" He replied, shaking his head "No, never have". A few months later, I attended a second weeklong retreat with Joe, where I had a private moment with him to discuss my experience at the airport. Joe said that it happens with his students often. And I thought I was special! Apparently, he explained, when we raise our vibration through meditation, or other modalities where we free ourselves from the dense thinking of the analytical mind, healing occurs. The vibrational patterns are so increased that the energy literally lights up our brain like a Christmas tree. We are energy systems. When we open ourselves to receive, when we pour ourselves into the spiritual mold, into the unknown space that pervades all things, is when the dense energy stored from the past releases through powerful emotions. This is when we can experience healing. If you haven't studied Joe Dispenza, or experienced his workshops, I encourage you to do so. He is the rock star of the meditation movement in the western world. The experience is both entertaining and enlightening with the added benefit of meeting like-minded people on the same journey of healing and awakening as you.

Are You Ready?

I recently contacted a close friend to wish him a happy birthday. I hadn't heard from him for several months, which was not unusual, as we were both living our own lives. When he answered the phone, his voice cracked. I asked him what was going on? My friend explained his journey with cancer, how he had isolated while he suffered the loneliness and pain of chemotherapy, the unknown, and the fear of leaving his family. My friend sounded softer, more humble and full of gratitude. He was more open and vulnerable, which only made me love him more. He was a different person because of deep suffering. Through suffering, we learn compassion for others and gratitude for the small things in life that previously we may have taken for granted. No matter what your standing in life, be it rich or poor, black or white (and all the colors in between) we are ALL destined to suffer. It's inevitable for every human life. The truth is the suffering makes us REAL. We're all going to die; the bigger question is how do you want to LIVE? My friend, at 62 years old, will no longer, in his words, waste any more precious time. He's going to survive this trauma and live a new life. He may not be religious, but he is being reborn. Many of you can relate to his pain. The good news is you don't have to wait for a tragic occurrence to wake up. Unfortunately, most people do. Something has to occur that shakes our world and forces us to make change. Then, and only then, do we pay proper attention to what really matters? It is up to us to pay attention to the signals and pick up the receiver before it's too late. There are choices that you have before the emergency bell rings in your own life. You don't have to continue to suppress emotions that may eventually kill you before your time. You can choose the inward path to your own healing, as I am suggesting in this book, or you can choose to stay in the same inherited life patterns, knowing that insanity is doing the same thing and expecting a different result!

Taking Action

You can learn to understand your nature through personality profiling, uncover hidden beliefs from childhood, go deeper into yourself through "Camera Talk", or other modalities to put space between yourself and your thoughts, partake of plant medicines and meditation retreats to experience the spiritual world that calls you to know more, and yet without testing yourself in the outer world, you will fall short of knowing who you are. You must take chances of yourself, and no longer stay hidden. In the next chapter, I explain how to overcome rejection, be bold to take chances of yourself and practice honing your gifts so that you can take your rightful place in the world, and become the healing force that you are.

Action Steps:

Talk to your camera or journal.

1. What have you learned from your most painful experiences?
2. What would you do differently knowing what you now know?
3. How could you help others avoid the pitfalls that you experienced?

The New Selfish

To Pour Myself into The Mold

When I pour myself into the mold
I free myself from all that is cold
And rigid as I unfold into the depths of my soul
I let go of all that is old
From a time gone past, from a time gone by
I free myself from every lie
The truth of life flows through my being
I become one with all that is worth feeling and seeing
When I pour myself into the mold
I release all that has been frozen and cold
My body, my soul, I am one with my goal
To let go of all past pain
To be in the moment my heavenly gain
For the mold is where the change takes place
When I give myself to its unending space
I am free to a new word spoken
Of love for myself, I become unbroken
By letting go into the space unknown
My true identity is revealed and shown
First to myself, as I am set free
I become one with my maker and so pleased is HE!

CHAPTER 9

"Virtue is bold, and goodness never fearful."

William Shakespeare

The Outward Journey

As we learn about our nature through personality profiling, unearth unconscious beliefs by self-examination, journey inward through contemplation, and apply these insights to become self-aware, we must test ourselves in the outer world to uncover our abilities and discover limitations. We must enter the arena of life, face our fears, and develop the gifts that lie within. We do this with practice and experimentation. Deciding who you want to become and making commitments towards those goals, and being bold enough to follow through will bring you up against yourself, where with practice and determination, you will experience a new level of awareness, a new sense of self. With persistence, you will overcome unconscious beliefs that had previously kept you stuck in mediocrity, or worse. By consistently taking the right actions, you will be reborn to the faith that has been waiting patiently on your arrival. Your ship comes in when you raise the anchor and set sail for new shores, where you can never go back to the place you came from. Then and only then do you own your story, where you use the past as lessons that were necessary for empathy and compassion, both for yourself as reference points, and for others as a teaching tool. There are no shortcuts to excellence. To discipline your gifts and harness the love of life that wants to pour through you is the gift that keeps giving. Not unlike learning to dance, developing your inherent gift takes time and practice. You must have patience with yourself and take the steps that will lead to your discovery and that which will set you free. Marrying the process, trusting in outcomes, and being present in the moments of self-discovery are the attitude strategies that will lighten your load and set you free from worry and anxiety. You are letting go of the old paradigm that has kept you "safe" by consciously entering a new path to self-discovery.

We can sit and meditate, talk to a camera, journal, partake of psychedelic medicines, do Yoga, Tai Chi, Chi Gong, read books, attend seminars and whatever other inward paths to journey into our inner world, and yet without demonstrations in the outer world we will feel lacking in our sense of contribution and accomplishments. We are here to give our gifts. In order to give our gift most effectively, we must practice taking chances of ourselves so we may overcome fears of rejection, abandonment, and of not being enough. The physiological experiences of rejection and that of abandonment are closely connected. It's an inherent fear that all humans come into the world experiencing. The moment we come through the birth canal and enter the cold, hard world is the first feeling of abandonment we experience. Out of the warmth and into the cold. Out you pop, a firm slap on your ass,

The New Selfish

and welcome to the world! My mother was in labor with me for three days, no cesarean deliveries back then. I knew what was coming. I didn't want to come out! The past, the birthing process, the first time we get dumped by our boyfriend or girlfriend, all of it is an initiation into overcoming the past and what we made it mean. That's why we must use our story as a learning tool to overcome the old self, which is the past. You do it by being BOLD. So how, especially for the introverted more fearful among us, do we overcome the illusion of not being enough, and overcome the fear of rejection? According to Jia Jiang, we do it by vaccination!

Rejection Proof

How do you vaccinate yourself against the feeling of not being enough or feeling rejected? If you practiced rejection as a learning tool, at some point you wouldn't care about being rejected. A shining example is a young man named Jia Jiang, who you can research on YouTube. Jia, originally from Beijing, had experiences as a young boy of feeling deeply rejected by his peers. His dream, when he moved to America, was to be an entrepreneur. He discovered he was dragging around the six-year-old child in his psyche that reminded him of not being enough, which affected his ability to speak up and have a voice. After moving to the United States, Jia knew his feelings of inadequacy were crippling his desires to move his career forward. He felt inadequate and unworthy of sharing his ideas, feeling stuck, destined to live an unfulfilled life. He changed his outcomes through radical honesty with himself, and bold intelligent commitments to overcome his deep-rooted fears. Whilst his commitments may at first sound unintelligent, they were, in fact, brilliant, enabling Jia to become an example of possibility to all of us stuck in the old self, afraid of rejection. After reading a book on rejection, Jia committed to 100 days of experiencing rejection. He reasoned that if he felt rejected enough times, eventually he would become immune to the feeling. He made a commitment to make this a practice, consequently writing a book on the subject, titled "Rejection Proof".

Jia's choices are a wonderful example of overcoming fears from past childhood experiences. He committed himself to make unusual requests of strangers so that he could feel the very thing he was most afraid of–being rejected. Jia recruited an assistant to film each experience, posting them on YouTube. In his first experiment, he approached a stranger, who was a security guard, requesting $100. The security guard, of course, said no. He also asked Jia why he had asked for $100? Feeling too nervous to give an answer, Jia ran away from the stranger while being filmed by his compatriot, which they later posted on YouTube. Even though he felt rejection and humiliation, he had achieved his goal. Each day, he continued to make unusual requests from strangers, experiencing rejection at every turn, posting the experiences on YouTube. As it was his intention to be rejected, and no longer his fear, he could overcome the rejections, and watch the recordings with his buddy, transforming his fear into fun. The irony is people began honoring his requests, even though they were ridiculous. Jia became quite famous, where one of his videos went viral on YouTube. He has been a guest on talk shows and also gave a TED Talk. Jia's life has never been the same since he made the commitment to practice rejection. He has also taught classes at a university on why rejection is necessary in order to build character. Jia Jiang's story is one of overcoming the past and the old self. What can you do to release yourself from old patterns?

Over time, and with enough experiences you can become the master of your life with unlimited potential. If you have unlimited choices, it is because you have grown to a place of mastery in your life, which is living life without limits. And it all started with making a commitment. We all know of the inspiring stories of successful men and women that heard the word "NO" many times before their first YES! You can learn from Jia's story and overcome fears of rejection by being present in the moment and practicing sharing your gift without attachments to outcomes. It takes practice and faith. If you stick with it, your life will never be the same; remembering you are doing what you do because you like and respect yourself as the person you are becoming.

Fortune Favors The BOLD

In the year 2000, after a successful business deal selling one of my products into Wal-Mart, I went on a Celebrity cruise along with my wife, her 3-year-old son and my friend Frank. Frank was my attorney, who I mentioned in a previous chapter, was an expert in understanding personality types using the Myers-Briggs personality theory. I wanted to take Frank on a cruise, as he was very helpful in assisting me with my business dealings. During the second day of the 14 day cruise, Frank asked if I would approach the cruise director to see if we could give workshops on understanding personality types. He suggested we name the workshop "Discover Your Celebrity Personality". The idea did not thrill me, as I wanted to relax after a busy work schedule. However, I put my resistance aside and approached the cruise director, named Jim Cannon. He was very enthusiastic and accommodating about my proposal and happy to oblige. Two days later, after the variety show, Jim announced to the passengers, "Dr. Frank Natter and Dave Cavill are giving a presentation on understanding your personality type. If you want to know why you do what you do, or why your spouse or kids are not always how you would like them to be, then visit with Frank and Dave tomorrow at 10AM. Details are in the daily program". He endorsed us without ever seeing the presentation, which surprised us both!

The next morning, Frank and I gave our first workshop to a crowded room eager to know more about themselves and their loved ones. After the presentation, I handed out questionnaires asking the audience to rate their experience and if they would recommend it to their friends and loved ones. We received 5 stars and rave reviews. People love to know about themselves. Towards the end of the cruise, I requested Jim write a letter of recommendation, which I could then take to the enrichment program director for Celebrity once back on shore. He happily obliged, thanking us for our excellent work. The reality was Frank did all the work; he did all the speaking. I handed out papers and sat quietly by while he worked his magic.

Once back in Miami, I contacted the head offices of Royal Caribbean and Celebrity cruise lines requesting a meeting with the enrichment program lecturer's department head. Dressed in my best suit, and if I say it myself, looking very polished and professional, I entered the office building where I was scheduled to meet the head of the enrichment program, an attractive woman in her mid-thirties. After a brief introduction along with presenting Jim's recommendation letter, the conversation went like this:

The New Selfish

Her: Thank you! I spoke with Jim Cannon this morning David, we would love to have you and your partner Frank present workshops on future cruises. When would you like to go?

Me: (feeling surprised at how easy this was going) Great! What have you got next month?

Her: We have several 7 days, 12 days, or 14 day cruises in the Caribbean, or you could do Alaska if you would prefer?

Me: (thinking this is great!) How about we do the 14-day in the Caribbean?

Her: OK great! (Pauses) I've got you scheduled for the 14 day cruise in the western and eastern Caribbean, three weeks from now. There's a $50 charge per cabin for each Enrichment program lecturer.

Me: You mean we have to pay?

Her: Yes, it's company policy that we charge a minimum of $50 per cabin per lecture.

Me: I don't mean to be disrespectful, but if you want quality presentations, surely it should likely be the other way around? With all due respect, I saw the other lectures and I didn't think they were of the highest quality. I certainly don't think we should have to pay? After all, you have seen the passengers' feedback and Jim's recommendation letter?

Her: (after a pause) OK David, we will make an exception. Your presentations were highly rated.

Me: Thank you! We won't disappoint! People love to discover themselves! We get our own cabin, right?

Her: Unfortunately, no. Because there are two of you, we only allow one cabin per lecture. You'll have to share a cabin with your partner, Frank. (Frank was 300 pounds and snored like a rhinoceros! There was no way I was going to share a cabin with him!)

Me: How many enrichment program lectures do you have per cruise?

Her: Normally, we have two per cruise.

Me: What if I did a separate lecture?

Her: (looking surprised) On what subject?

Me: Hypnosis, I'm an expert on hypnosis! (I had taken a weekend class 10 years previously on hypnosis. I had never hypnotized a person in my life!)

Her: You do hypnosis?

Me: Yes! I've been practicing for years! People love it!

Her: Oh, I bet with that English accent–I'm sure people love you. That would be great! How exciting! On the longer cruises, such as the one I just booked you and Frank on, you would have to have a minimum of four presentations each an hour long, is that ok?

Me: Yes! I can do stress reduction, weight loss, smoking cessation and confidence for people that need to feel more sure about themselves. (Which was me! I realized what I was getting myself into? I'd hypnotized no one in my life!)

Her: Well, in that case, you can have your own cabin. You're all booked for three weeks from now on the 14-day through the western and eastern Caribbean.

The New Selfish

Me: OK, great! Oh, by the way can I sell CDs to people who attend my lectures?

Her: No, unfortunately we don't allow any selling to take place. The lectures are free - we don't want to give people the wrong impressions by placing pressure on them to purchase something.

Me: Umm, yes, I understand. The thing is hypnosis is a practice, and like any other practice, it takes time to adopt new habits. For lasting change to take place, it's necessary to recondition the subconscious mind. It takes at least 30 days to change a habit. I don't think we would serve your passengers if we didn't give them the opportunity to take the experience home with them. (I had a light bulb moment) Plus! When they are listening to the CD's it will remind them of Celebrity when they're thinking of booking their next cruise. (I was thinking - I'm good at this!)

Her: Umm, I see - Let me make a phone call. (She talks on the phone to her boss). OK then, great! You supply the CDs - you can sell them at the lecture and also in the gift shop. You keep 70% and we keep 30%. Is that acceptable?

Me: (thinking, f**** aye!) Yes! Great!

I got up from my chair, shook hands with my new best friend, and headed down the corridor. I pressed the elevator button and entered the elevator. That was when it hit me! What did I just do? How am I going to hypnotize people? I had three weeks to figure it out.

In the following three weeks prior to my inaugural cruise as an Enrichment Program Lecturer, I read as many books as I could on Hypnosis. I dug up notes from the weekend seminar

The New Selfish

I had attended 10 years previously, copied the scripts, located a recording studio and made CDs titled "Hypnosis at Sea". Three weeks later, after boarding the Celebrity Horizon, feeling sick and afraid, I approached the theater of the ship, where I would deliver my first and possibly last presentation on hypnosis. At the entryway of the theater, propped on an artist's easel, was an enormous poster with my picture: "David Cavill, Entrepreneur and Master Hypnotist". I looked at me, peering back at me. "He" didn't look worried. "He" was handsome, rugged, fearless, a winner! Why wasn't I feeling like "him"? "Him" in the poster, looking back at me. I was at war with myself, angry with the poster child looking back at me. Drip, drip, the sweat was rolling downs my armpits, cold and wet. I wanted to run away... I couldn't. The ship, as they say, had sailed, and I was on it. Fuck! Is this really happening? Cold, terrified, wet with sweat, nervous with trepidation, I stood at the entranceway of the theater looking at the image of myself. It wasn't narcissism that I was feeling gazing at the handsome, assured image that was I. That was not who I was. I was a fake! I stood at the doorway to the upcoming entranceway to hell, paralyzed with fear, the lost child with nowhere to go. Where was my momma now? There was no way out. Frank, smooth and assured, was in a separate room ready to give his presentation on personality types. Perhaps his snoring wouldn't have been so bad after all, I thought. Snoring? That was heaven compared to this! What was I thinking? I was desperately hoping it would be a beautiful sunny day, the passengers sunning themselves on the open deck, hoping, praying no one would show up to see me fluff my lines and drown in my puddle of toxic sweat. I peered through the outer porthole close to where I was standing. Rain! It was raining! I paced back and forth in a separate room, hiding from the throng of passengers entering the theatre, checking out the self-assured master hypnotist poster child as they walked through the door. I was sunk! (No pun intended) doomed! My "ship" was going down! This is how it must've felt on the Titanic, is what I was thinking, those poor bastards. Fear took me over. "I could jump? The Caribbean is warm". I was rambling, pacing back and forth. Talking to myself, "You're not jumping! You don't have the guts!"

My first presentation was on stress reduction! "Get a grip, you idiot, get a grip!" I was about to face a terrible fate. I straightened my back, took a deep breath, and entered the theatre. It was bucketing down outside. The house was full, awaiting the "Master Hypnotist". There was no turning back now.

Turn On Your Heart Light

The difference between excitement and fear is imperceptibly small. The biological symptoms are almost identical to how these two emotions can make us feel. Anxiety and excitement are both arousal emotions. In both, the heart beats faster, cortisol surges, and the body prepares for action. They are "arousal congruent". The only difference is excitement is a positive emotion within anticipation that things can go well, whereas anxiety is a fear of upcoming dread. When there's no way out, we have a choice as to turn the light switch on, towards excitement, or to turn it off into darkness, which is fear. It's a decision, a choice. Neil diamond sings it best with his song "Heart light". Neil sings; "Turn on your heart light, let it make a happy glow, let it shine wherever you go, for all the world to see". After a glowing introduction by the cruise director, cold sweat dripping down my beautiful dark

The New Selfish

blue silk shirt, I bounded onto the stage to begin my career as a Master Hypnotist. I was going to teach these poor bastards how to have less stress, even if it killed me! After all, it takes one to know one! The cruise director had made his way to the back of the room, where he was watching intently. I turned my attention to the cruise director, requesting the passengers give him a round of applause for his hard work and dedication.

I began my first "Hypnosis At Sea" presentation, explaining why and how Hypnosis worked, hoping somehow it would work its magic on me! After a few minutes, the cruise director gave me a smile and thumbs up, whereupon he vacated the room. After my initial 20-minute introduction, I disappeared into the sound room where I dimmed the lights, pressed, "play" on the studio CD machine and heard my voice echo through the room. I watched as the passengers relaxed and went into deep relaxation. All hypnosis is self-hypnosis. They were on a cruise; they wanted to relax. My voice, combined with the background ocean waves threaded into the recording, was all they needed. They loved it! I was on my way. At the conclusion of the presentation, after answering questions from the audience, and selling 20 CD packages, I returned to my cabin and cried.

Upon my return to the mainland, and safely back in Tampa, I opened a small office in my friend's massage studio, placed ads in the local newspaper and began practicing hypnosis. I didn't want to sweat like that ever again. The clients I worked with in that small office in Clearwater, Florida, came to me for smoking cessation, weight loss, fingernail biting, insomnia, and other ailments. I never claimed to be a doctor and my clients never asked. You can't be a prophet in your own land. You can be one in someone else's. I sold CDs to the passengers who attended my

The New Selfish

lectures aboard Celebrity cruise line ships averaging approximately $2000 in profit per cruise. I overcome my own deep-seated fears and travelled the world doing so. I met fascinating people and have many stories based on my experience as an enrichment program lecturer. One of which was where I met Regis Philbin, (now sadly deceased) the well-known talk show host. His wife Joy had attended one of my presentations the day before. Joy shared her experience from the previous day, where apparently she had enjoyed my presentation and recommended Regis should attend my next lecture. I never encouraged people to attend my lectures because I never quite lost the feeling of being a fake. I explained to Regis that he didn't need to attend my weight loss lecture and I would happily provide him with my CDs. He said he was decided on attending my lecture and nothing was going to keep him away, and was looking forward to the experience. Two days later, Regis quietly entered the theatre with Joy taking a seat at the back of the room. Regis fell asleep during the lecture, mouth wide open, gently snoring. The next evening, while at my dining table, Regis approached, requesting if he could have a private moment? I excused myself to my guests, whereupon Regis and I made our way over to an area of the restaurant hidden from the many interested eyes. Regis explained he was having difficulty sleeping, constantly referring to me as "Doctor". I immediately reminded him he didn't have a sleep problem during my presentation! His eyes lit up with recognition. "Joy couldn't believe how well I slept!" We both laughed. The next evening, I gifted Regis a CD package. I will never know how many times my voice lulled Regis to sleep. He's no longer with us, sleeping peacefully, I hope, in the afterlife. I travelled the world in style, escorting family members and friends along with me on the ride. I met many interesting people of whom I have many stories, all because I placed myself in the unknown and took a chance.

Pushing The Envelope

During my tenure as an enrichment lecturer, I approached a company named "Elemis" who operated spas on the cruise ships around the world. I had the idea that the spa company could offer hypnosis as a treatment for the passengers whilst on their cruise. I presented the idea to the Board of Directors in Coral Gables, Miami. They received the idea warmly where we agreed on a first sail date for hypnosis treatments on board a Royal Caribbean ship, which was the largest ship in the world. I hired a professional hypnotist who would be the trainer for my company. Elemis produced 5000 of my CDs ready for its inaugural cruise offering "Hypnosis at Sea." Unfortunately, two days prior to sailing, the COO reneged on his verbal agreement and would not sign a non-compete agreement and the opportunity was never realized. Somewhere, I don't know where, there are 5000 "Hypnosis at Sea" CDs with my voice in a warehouse that never saw the light of day, or experienced the ocean waves. For the record, no one hypnotizes you but you. Hypnotists are coaches giving permission and guidance to enable their client to experience their own inner world. If you really want to grow beyond the old self and overcome your patterns from the past, you must take steps to enter the arena. Your actions do not have to be like those of Jia overcoming rejection, or myself as a "hypnotist", or even more extreme, the teenager Frank Abagnale portrayed by Leonardo DiCaprio in the movie "Catch Me If You Can". However, to realize your potential, you must put yourself in a place where you

The New Selfish

have no choice but to show up and be bold. I have learned that showing up is half the battle. You can only discover yourself in the arena, not standing on the sidelines of life. You can best do this by planning a strategy with intelligent plans and commitments, and then following through. Whatever you decide to do, do it for you. While others may be the benefactors of your bold choices, the nucleus is you.

The Thing

The thing is never the thing; it never is
It's the journey to get to the thing that makes it what it is
If you think once you get there, all will be well
You may find that empty space is a trap made in hell
Then you missed the whole point...
It's the journey you see
The journey is where you make yourself free
For you are with yourself clear to the end
When you marry your journey
You are your best friend

Never disappointed and nothing to fear
Without expectations, you'll have good cheer
It's even better doing what you love
The moments are many from the sweet man above
Giving it your all, you do answer your call
To partner with your maker, a heavenly ball

So travel light, and travel well
Keep your eye on the road with the virtues you know
Destiny will take care of if itself
When you place the expectation on some far away shelf.

"Fall Down Seven times, Stand Up Eight"

Japanese Proverb

50 Famous People Who Failed At First

Not everyone who's on top today got there with success after success. More often than not, those who history best remember were faced with obstacles that forced them to work harder and show more determination than others. They showed up, and didn't give up. It may surprise you at the examples of courageous men and women cited below and their pathway to success.

Business Gurus

These business executives and the companies they founded are today known around the world, but as these stories show, their beginnings weren't always smooth.

1. Henry Ford:
    While Ford is today known for his innovative assembly line and American-made cars, he wasn't an instant success. In fact, his early businesses failed and left him

broke five times before he founded the successful Ford Motor Company.

2. R. H. Macy:

   Most people are familiar with this large department store chain, but Macy didn't always have it easy. Macy started seven failed businesses before finally hitting big with his store in New York City.

3. F. W. Woolworth:

   Some may not know this name today, but Woolworth was once one of the biggest names in department stores in the U.S. Before starting his own business, Woolworth worked at a dry goods store and was not allowed to wait on customers because his boss said he lacked the sense needed to do so.

4. Soichiro Honda:

   The billion-dollar business that is Honda began with a series of failures and fortunate turns of luck. Honda was turned down by Toyota Motor Corporation after interviewing for a job as an engineer, leaving him jobless for quite some time. He started making scooters of his own at home, and spurred on by his neighbors, finally started his own business.

5. Akio Morita:

   You may not have heard of Morita, but you've undoubtedly heard of his company, Sony. Sony's first product was a rice cooker that unfortunately didn't cook rice so much as burn it, selling less than 100 units. This first setback didn't stop Morita and his partners as they pushed forward to create a multi-billion dollar company.

6. Bill Gates:

    Gates didn't seem like a shoo-in for success after dropping out of Harvard and starting a failed first business with Microsoft co-founder Paul Allen called Traf-O-Data. While this early idea didn't work, Gates later work created the global empire that is Microsoft.

7. Harland David Sanders:

    Perhaps better known as Colonel Sanders of Kentucky Fried Chicken fame, Sanders had a hard time selling his chicken at first. In fact, his famous secret chicken recipe was rejected 1,009 times before a restaurant accepted it.

8. Walt Disney:

    Today Disney rakes in billions from merchandise, movies and theme parks around the world, but Walt Disney himself had a bit of a rough start. A newspaper editor fired him because, "he lacked imagination and had no good ideas." After that, Disney started several businesses that didn't last too long and ended with bankruptcy and failure. He kept plugging along, however, and eventually found a recipe for success that worked.

Scientists and Thinkers

9. Albert Einstein:

    Most of us take Einstein's name as synonymous with genius, but he didn't always show such promise. Little Albert Einstein did not speak until he was four and did not read until he was seven, causing his teachers and parents to think he was mentally handicapped, slow and anti-social. Eventually, he was expelled from school and was refused admittance to the Zurich Polytechnic School. It might have taken him a bit longer but most people would agree that he caught on pretty well in the end, winning the Nobel Prize and changing the face of modern physics.

10. Charles Darwin:

In his early years, Darwin gave up on having a medical career and was often chastised by his father for being lazy and too dreamy. Darwin himself wrote, "I was considered by all my masters and my father, a very ordinary boy, rather below the common standard of intellect." Perhaps they judged too soon, as Darwin today is well known for his scientific studies.

11. Robert Goddard:

Goddard today is hailed for his research and experimentation with liquid-fueled rockets, but during his lifetime, his ideas were often rejected and mocked by his scientific peers who thought they were outrageous and impossible. Today rocket and space travel don't seem far-fetched at all, due largely in part to the work of this scientist who worked against the feelings of the time.

12. Isaac Newton:

Newton was undoubtedly a genius with math, but he had some failings early on. He never did particularly well in school and when put in charge of running the family farm, he failed miserably, so poorly in fact that an uncle took charge and sent him off to Cambridge, where he finally blossomed into the scholar we know today.

13. Socrates:

Despite leaving no written records behind, Socrates is one of the greatest philosophers of the Classical era. Because of his new ideas, in his own time, he was called "an immoral corrupter of youth" and was sentenced to death. Socrates didn't let this stop him and kept right on teaching until he was forced to poison himself.

14. Robert Sternberg:

This big name in psychology received a C in his first college introductory psychology class with his teacher telling him that, "there was already a famous Sternberg in psychology and it was obvious there would not be another." Sternberg showed him, however, graduating from Stanford with exceptional distinction in psychology, summa cum laude, and Phi Beta Kappa and eventually becoming the President of the American Psychological Association.

Inventors

15. Thomas Edison:

In his early years, teachers told Edison he was "too stupid to learn anything." Work was no better. He was fired from his first two jobs for not being productive enough. Even as an inventor, Edison made 1,000 unsuccessful attempts at inventing the light bulb. Of course, all those unsuccessful attempts finally resulted in the design that worked.

16. Orville and Wilbur Wright:

These brothers battled depression and family illness before starting the bicycle shop that would lead them to experimenting with flight. After many attempts at creating flying machines, several years of hard work, and tons of failed prototypes, the brothers finally created a plane that could get airborne and stay there.

Public Figures

17. Winston Churchill:

This Nobel Prize-winning, twice-elected Prime Minister of the United Kingdom wasn't always as well regarded as he is today. Churchill struggled in school and failed the sixth grade. After school, he faced many years of political failures, and was defeated in every election for public office until he finally became the Prime Minister at the ripe old age of 62.

18. Abraham Lincoln:

While today he is remembered as one of the greatest leaders of our nation, Lincoln's life wasn't so easy. In his youth, he went to war a captain and returned a private (if you're not familiar with military ranks, just know that private is as low as it goes.) Lincoln didn't stop failing there, however. He started many failed businesses and was defeated in many runs he made for public office.

19. Oprah Winfrey:

Most people know Oprah as one of the most iconic faces on TV, as well as one of the richest and most successful women in the world. Oprah faced a hard road to get to that position, however, enduring a rough and often abusive childhood and many career setbacks, including being fired from her job as a television reporter because she was "unfit for TV."

The New Selfish

20. Harry S. Truman:

    This WWI vet, Senator, Vice President and eventual President eventually found success in his life, but not without a few missteps along the way. Truman started a store that sold silk shirts and other clothing–seemingly a success at first–only to go bankrupt a few years later.

21. Dick Cheney:

    This Vice President and business executive made his way to the White House but flunked out of Yale University, not once, but twice. Former President George W. Bush joked with Cheney about this, stating, "So now we know–if you graduate from Yale, you become president. If you drop out, you get to be vice president."

Entertainers

22. Jerry Seinfeld:

    Just about everybody knows who Seinfeld is, but the first time the young comedian walked on stage at a comedy club, he looked out at the audience, froze, and was eventually jeered and booed off of the stage. Seinfeld knew he could do it, so he went back the next night, completed his set to laughter and applause, and the rest is history.

23. Fred Astaire:

    In his first screen test, the testing director of MGM noted that Astaire "Can't act, can't sing, slightly bald, can dance a little." Astaire became an incredibly successful actor, singer and dancer and kept that note in his Beverly Hills home to remind him of where he came from.

24. Sidney Poitier:

After his first audition, the casting director told Poitier, "Why don't you stop wasting people's time and go out and become a dishwasher or something?" Poitier vowed to show him he could make it, winning an Oscar and become one of the most well-regarded actors in the business.

25. Jeanne Moreau:

As a young actress just starting out, a casting director told this French actress that she was simply not pretty enough to make it in films. He couldn't have been more wrong as Moreau went on to star in nearly 100 films.

26. Charlie Chaplin:

It's hard to imagine film without the iconic Charlie Chaplin, but Hollywood studio chiefs initially rejected his act because they felt it was a little too nonsensical to ever sell!

27. Lucille Ball:

During her career, Ball had thirteen Emmy nominations and four wins, also earning the Lifetime Achievement from the Kennedy Center Honors. Before starring in I Love Lucy, she was regarded as a failed actress and a B movie star. Even her drama instructors didn't feel she could make it, telling her to try another profession. She, of course, proved them all wrong.

28. Harrison Ford:

In his first film, Ford was told by the movie execs that he simply didn't have what it takes to be a star. Today, with many hits under his belt, iconic portrayals of characters like Han Solo and Indiana Jones, and a career that stretches decades, Ford can proudly show that he does, in fact, have what it takes.

29. Marilyn Monroe:

While Monroe's star burned out early, she had a period of outstanding success in her life. Despite a rough upbringing and being told by modeling agents she should be a secretary, Monroe became a pin-up, model and actress that still strikes a chord with people today.

30. Oliver Stone:

This Oscar-winning filmmaker began his first novel while at Yale, a project that eventually caused him to fail out of school. This would be a poor decision as the text was rejected, eventually being published 1998, at which time it was not well-received. After dropping out of school, Stone moved to Vietnam to teach English, later enlisting in the army and fighting in the war, a battle that earned him two Purple Hearts and helped him find the inspiration for his later work that often centered on war.

Writers and Artists

31. Vincent Van Gogh:

During his lifetime, Van Gogh sold only one painting, and this was to a friend and only for a small amount of money. While Van Gogh was never a success during his life, he plugged on with painting, sometimes starving to complete his over 800 known works. Today, they bring in hundreds of millions.

The New Selfish

32. Emily Dickinson:

Recluse and poet Emily Dickinson is a commonly read and loved writer. Yet in her lifetime she was all but ignored, having fewer than a dozen poems published out of her almost 1,800 completed works.

33. Theodor Seuss Geisel:

Today, nearly every child has read The Cat in the Hat or Green Eggs and Ham, yet 27 different publishers rejected Dr. Seuss's first book; "To Think That I Saw It on Mulberry Street".

34. Charles Schultz:

Schultz's Peanuts comic strip has had enduring fame, yet this cartoonist had every cartoon he submitted rejected by his high school yearbook staff. Even after high school, Schultz didn't have it easy, applying and being rejected for a position working with Walt Disney.

35. Steven Spielberg:

While today Spielberg's name is synonymous with big budget, they rejected him from the University of the Southern California School of Theater, Film and Television three times. He eventually attended school at another location, only to drop out to become a director before finishing. Thirty-five years after starting his degree, Spielberg returned to school in 2002 to complete his work and earn his BA.

36. Stephen King:

The first book by this author, the iconic thriller Carrie, received 30 rejections, finally causing King to give up and throw it in the trash. His wife fished it out and encouraged him to resubmit it. And the rest is history with King now having hundreds of books published the distinction of being one of the best-selling authors of all time.

37. Zane Grey:

Incredibly popular in the early 20th century, this adventure book writer began his career as a dentist, something he quickly hated. So, he wrote, only to see rejection after rejection for his works, being told eventually that he had no business being a writer and should give up. It took him years, but at 40, Zane finally got his first work published, leaving him with almost 90 books to his name and selling over 50 million copies worldwide.

38. J. K. Rowling:

Rowling may be rolling in a lot of Harry Potter dough today, but before she published the series of novels, she was nearly penniless, severely depressed, divorced, trying to raise a child on her own while attending school and writing a novel. Rowling went from depending on welfare to survive to being one of the richest women in the world in only five years through her hard work and determination.

39. Monet:

Today, Monet's work sells for millions of dollars and hangs in some of the most prestigious institutions in the world. Yet during his own time he was mocked and rejected by the artistic elite, the Paris Salon. Monet kept at his impressionist style, which caught on and was a starting point for some major changes to art that ushered in the modern era.

40. Jack London:

This well-known American author wasn't always such a success. While he would publish popular novels like "White Fang" and "The Call of the Wild", his first story received six hundred rejection slips before finally being accepted.

41. Louisa May Alcott:

Most people are familiar with Alcott's most famous work, Little Women. Yet Alcott faced a bit of a battle to get her work out there and was encouraged to find work as a servant by her family to make ends meet. It was her letters back home during her experience as a nurse in the Civil War that gave her the first big break she needed.

Musicians

42. Wolfgang Amadeus Mozart:

Mozart began composing at the age of five, writing over 600 pieces of music that we laud today as some of the best created. Yet during his lifetime, Mozart didn't have such an easy time, and was often restless, leading to his dismissal from a position as a court musician in Salzburg. He struggled to keep the support of the aristocracy and died with little to his name.

43. Elvis Presley:

As one of the best-selling artists of all time, Elvis has become a household name even years after his death. But back in 1954, Elvis was still a nobody, and Jimmy Denny, manager of the Grand Ole Opry, fired Elvis Presley after just one performance, telling him, "You're going nowhere, son. You ought to go back to driving a truck."

44. Igor Stravinsky:

   In 1913, when Stravinsky debuted his now famous Rite of Spring, audiences rioted, running the composer out of town. Yet it was this very work that changed the way composers in the 19th century thought about music and cemented his place in musical history.

45. The Beatles:

   Few people can deny the lasting power of this super group, still popular with listeners around the world today. Yet when they were just starting out, a recording company told them no. They were told, "we don't like their sound, and guitar music is on the way out," two things the rest of the world couldn't have disagreed with more.

46. Ludwig van Beethoven:

   In his formative years, young Beethoven was incredibly awkward on the violin and was often so busy working on his own compositions that he neglected to practice. Despite his love of composing, his teachers felt he was hopeless at it and would never succeed with the violin or in composing. Beethoven kept plugging along, however, and composed some of the best-loved symphonies of all time–five of them while he was completely deaf.

Athletes

47. Michael Jordan:

   Most people wouldn't believe that a man often lauded as the best basketball player of all time was cut from his high school basketball team. Luckily, Jordan didn't let this setback stop him from playing the game and he has stated,

"I have missed over 9,000 shots in my career. I have lost almost 300 games. On 26 occasions, I have been entrusted to take the game winning shot, and I missed. I have failed over and over and over again in my life. And that is why I succeed."

48. Stan Smith:

This tennis player was rejected from even being a lowly ball boy for a Davis Cup tennis match because event organizers felt he was too clumsy and uncoordinated. Smith proved them wrong, showcasing his not-so-clumsy skills by winning Wimbledon, U. S. Open and eight Davis Cups.

49. Babe Ruth:

You probably know Babe Ruth because of his home run record (714 during his career), but along with all those home runs came a pretty hefty amount of strikeouts as well (1,330 in all). In fact, for decades, he held the record for strikeouts. When asked about this, he simply said, "Every strike brings me closer to the next home run."

50. Tom Landry:

As the coach of the Dallas Cowboys, Landry brought the team two Super Bowl victories, five NFC Championship victories and holds the record for the most career wins. He also has the distinction of having one of the worst first seasons on record (winning no games) and winning five or fewer over the next four seasons.

You Can Do It!

When you truly value yourself, you will make the commitments, do the work, overcome adversities, and follow through to what lies waiting for you on the other side, because YOU are worth it.

Sources

POEMS:

Because I Know The Soul of You – David Cavill

Man in The Glass - Author Unknown

Being Creative - David Cavill

The Messenger - David Cavill

The Man In The Tree - David Cavill

Decisions - David Cavill

The Road Less Travelled - David Cavill

To Pour Myself Into The Mold - David Cavill

The Thing - David Cavill

INTRODUCTION

Association of psychology science – Volpe, Kate. 2003 "False Memory"

Forgive them for they no not what they are doing. Luke 23:34

Selfish definition: Merriam Webster

CHAPTER 1

Trans generational memory: Neuroscience Magazine. Zhan, Sarah.

Dr. Rechavi, Oded. TED talk 2020

Stern, Larry. Dr. Dias, Brian. Prof Pembrey, Marcus.

Nature neuroscience journal. Emory University School of Medicine.

Emerson, Ralph. I like the silent church before the service begins, better than any preaching." Good Reads.

Amistad – Joseph Cinque. Wikipedia

National Archives 2021 "The Amistad Case"

CHAPTER 2

Socrates "Know Yourself " Unexamined Life – Wikipedia

MBTI Personality test. MBTIonline.com

Fonda, Jane. Good Reads 2015

Reticular activation system. RAS. Science Direct. Wikipedia. Study.com

Metacognition. Queens University. Pintrich, P.R 2002

CHAPTER 3

Dr. Love, John. Scripps Health San Diego CA

Pannikin Coffee and Tea Encinitas CA

Guilt Article- Psychology today 2022

Norwegian Prison System. The Journal 2014. Business Insider 2014.

Failure rates: Wilkinson & Finkbeiner. Daily Beast. US bureau of labor.

Singer, Michael. The Surrender Experiment. Harmony, Rodale. 2015

60,000 – 80,000 thoughts per day. Brain facts. Healthybrains.org

Coelho, Paulo "The Alchemist" Harper Torch 1988

Tolle, Ekhart "The Power of Now" Namaste 1997

Tolle, Ekhart "A New Earth" Dutton 2005

CHAPTER 4

RAS-Reticular Activation System. Van Schneider, Tobias 2017

Study.com University of Minnesota 2022

Dalio, Ray. "Principles" Simon and Schuster 2017

Robbins, Anthony. Date with Destiny. Tonyrobbins.com

Tzu, Lao. World History Encyclopedia

Byrne, Rhonda "The Secret" Simon and Schuster 2006

Hill, Napoleon. "Think and Grow Rich" 1937

CHAPTER 5

Brown, Brene. "The Power of Vulnerability" TED Talk 2013

Hemmingway, Ernest. "A Farewell To Arms" Scribner 1929

Simon and Schuster 1995

Sadhguru "The Power of Willingness" YouTube 2021

CHAPTER 6

Watts, Alan. Idea pod.

Life and Whim. "The Boy and the Butterfly" 2018.

Angiyou, Lydia. The Globe 2006

Cavallo, Angela. Springfield Genealogy bank 1982

Holtrust, Kyle. Arizona Daily. 2006

Harris, Nick. Wichita Eagle Star. 2009

Sicolo, Abigail. Daily Mail 2009

McNamee, Donna. Daily Mail. 2009

Dali Lama. "The Art of Happiness" Easton Press. 1998

Intimacy. IN-TO-ME-SEE Marriage.com 2020

Williams, Robin. "Dead Poets Society" 1989

Sinek, Simon. "Why" TED Talk. 2016

CHAPTER 7

Campbell, Joseph. "The Hero With A Thousand Faces" Bollingen 1949

Heart Beat. Blood stats. Temple Health. 2021

Free Association therapy. Study.com 2021. Better Help. 2023

Dyer, Wayne. "Getting in The Gap. Hay House. 2006

Shawshank Redemption. Movie 1994. Castel Rock.

CHAPTER 8

Robbins, Anthony. 6 Human needs. Tonyrobbins.com

PTSD. Suicide facts. Truffle Report.

Spectrum News. 2021

"Shock To Awe" Movie. Amazon

"New Life Ayahuasca" Ayahuasca Retreat, Costa Rica

Dispenza, Joe. Meditation retreats. Drjoedispenza.com

CHAPTER 9

Jiang, Jia. "Rejection Proof" Harmony 2015

Anxiety and Excitement. Greatest.com 2021

Famously Successful People. Addicted 2 Success 2011

Success Consciousness.

ABOUT THE AUTHOR

David Cavill is originally from the United Kingdom, now residing in Asheville, North Carolina. He has spent his lifetime studying personal growth and development, attending Tony Robbins' events, Dr. Joe Dispenza meditation retreats, breath work workshops, Ayahuasca retreats, Myers Briggs personality profiling, ministerial studies, and many other personal development retreats to understand human behavior. He is a trained workshop facilitator and avid researcher and poet. David developed the philosophies in these writings by studying spiritual teachers such as Eckhart Tolle, Wayne Dyer, Sadhguru, Joel Osteen, Alan Watts, Deepak Chopra, Abraham Hicks and others. He is also the originator of "Camera Talk" a methodology to know your true self more intimately.

David is a successful entrepreneur and the holder of several United States and Canadian patents. His products have featured on QVC and HSN, and distributed through retail giants such as Wal-Mart and Home Depot. He has been featured in Infomercials; hosted local TV and radio shows titled "Success" and served as an enrichment lecturer teaching self-hypnosis and positivity.

In "The New Selfish" David has distilled his studies and experiences into simple exercises at the end of each chapter enabling the reader to uncover their purpose. He shares stories as metaphors on how to overcome debilitating habits and thought patterns, encouraging the reader to awaken to their true identity and live a purposeful and productive life. You can contact David at www.Davidcavill.com

Printed in Great Britain
by Amazon